DCHS *Year Book* • Volume 87 (2008)

DUTCHESS COUNTY HISTORICAL SOCIETY
YEAR BOOK 2008

Poetry
in
Dutchess
County

SELECTED AND INTRODUCED BY
HOLLY WAHLBERG

Dutchess County Historical Society

DUTCHESS COUNTY HISTORICAL SOCIETY YEAR BOOK 2008
Volume 87 • Published annually since 1915

Published by Dutchess County Historical Society
Clinton House, 549 Main Street, Poughkeepsie, New York
Mailing Address: DCHS, P.O. Box 88, Poughkeepsie, New York 12602
dchistorical@verizon.net; www.dutchesscountyhistoricalsociety.org
Individual copies may be purchased through the Historical Society.
Selected earlier Year Books are also available for purchase.

ISSN 0739-8565
ISBN 978-0-944733-03-5

Manufactured in the United States of America

CALL FOR ARTICLES

The 2009 Year Book, *Reflections on a River*, will celebrate the Hudson River in Dutchess County history to honor the 2009 Hudson-Fulton-Champlain Quadricentennial. Articles should pertain to the Hudson River and its relationship to Dutchess County's history in such areas as art, literature, science, industry, architecture, recreation, politics, commerce, national, regional or local events, or other aspects of Dutchess County life. Deadline for submission: May 1, 2009.

Articles should be in Microsoft Word format between 2,000 and 10,000 words in length. Authors are encouraged to provide illustrations with their text. Electronic submissions of photos or other illustrations are welcome in JPEG format at a minimum of 300 dpi. Images should be accompanied by detailed captions. All permissions to publish images are the responsibility of the author. Please include 3-4 sentences of biographical information for the list of contributors. Acceptance for publication is at the discretion of the editor and the DCHS Publications Committee.

Authors should send: One double spaced typescript paper copy (please remember to also include photo captions and a 3-4 sentence author biography) *and* one CD-R containing article, captions and biographical information as a MS Word document (please also include JPEG's of illustrations or photos at a minimum of 300 dpi). Please mail to: Year Book Editor, Dutchess County Historical Society, P.O. Box 88, Poughkeepsie, NY 12602.

The Historical Society encourages accuracy but does not assume responsibility for statements of fact or opinion made by contributors.

Contents

(Written for the Dutchess County Historical Society Banquet, 1935)

Hail to Old Dutchess

James M. DeGarmo

All hail to Old Dutchess, the land of our birth,
The dearest, the grandest old county on earth!
Her daughters the fairest, her mothers the best;
Her fathers and sons have a heritage blest!

Her patriots' glory her annals proclaim,
And the pages of history shine with her fame;
While her sons boast so proudly, wherever they roam,
"We remember our mother, Old Dutchess, our home."

They fought for our banner, the Red, White and Blue,
Which waves o'er no children more loyal and true;
Not one of her boys lives, but with colors unfurled,
Will strike for Old Dutchess, against the whole world.

How we loved her, we boys, in the days long ago,
With a love that our manhood will never forego;
We all have grown old, and in some ways more wise,
Still Dutchess, Old Dutchess, is first in our eyes.

And amid all the toil and struggle of life,
When o'erwrought with its maddening contention and strife,
How we long for the sweet rest our young hearts have known,
'Ere we wandered away from Old Dutchess our home.

How softly the sunlight drops down on her hills,
How sweetly her valleys with loveliness fills;
How blue is the sky that bends over her fields,
And smiles on the harvest her fertile soil yields!

How murmur her brooklets, so rippling and clear,
While the youth and the maiden are lingering near!
How we love every spot in her time honored soil,
Where we learned that true manhood, the manhood of toil.

And dearer today is the home of our love,
More precious each year do its memories prove;
While the longing grows deeper, the farther we roam,
To wander once more in Old Dutchess, our home.

So tonight in our hearts, her high altar we raise,
And we lay on it gratitude, honor and praise;
Let our spirits rejoice, let our voices all ring,
As the glories of Dutchess, Old Dutchess we sing.

And together, as firm in our friendship we stand,
With heart linked to heart and hand joined to hand;
We solemnly swear, that whatever may come,
We forever will cherish Old Dutchess, our home.

Henry A. Livingston
(1748-1828)

In 1771, Henry Livingston received, as an advance on his inheritance, 333 acres of land comprising the southern end of his father's estate Linlithgow, immediately south of the village of Poughkeepsie. To this new estate, which he named Locust Grove, he brought his bride Sarah (and later, his second wife, Jane) and spent the next 57 years here as a prosperous farmer, sawmill operator, surveyor, mapmaker, Revolutionary War major, father to 12 children, and possibly father to a 13th: the American Santa Claus.

Since 1860, descendants of Henry Livingston, Jr. have asserted that one of the world's most famous poems "A Visit from Saint Nicholas" (more commonly known as "The Night Before Christmas") was not written by Clement Clarke Moore but rather by their ancestor, an obscure Poughkeepsie farmer named Henry Livingston. Each generation of Livingstons has carried the burden of keeping alive this claim, even though most literary scholars considered it little more than a quaint, if intriguing, family legend.

The mystery centers on Henry Livingston, whom evidence clearly shows was a marvelous fellow - fond of joyful music, drawing, dancing, sleighing parties, and the writing of light-hearted verses for children. Clement Clarke Moore, on the other hand, was a misanthropic Bible scholar (even his mother found him grim) whose stern writings bear little if any resemblance to the rollicking Christmas poem.[1]

The controversy has always had all the elements of a very good story. In 1927, *The New Yorker* magazine sent a young writer named James Thurber to investigate (Thurber agreed with the Livingston contingent, then rewrote the poem "in the Ernest Hemingway manner" - a parody which has itself become a Christmas classic).[2]

In 1958, Vassar College president Henry Noble MacCracken became a celebrated convert to the Livingston authorship theory, noting confidently, "The world will come around in time, no use hurrying..."[3] And it seemed the world was indeed in no hurry.

In 2000, authorial attribution expert and Vassar College Professor Don Foster agreed to work with two Livingston descendants on reopening the authorship debate. Foster's findings, favoring Livingston rather than Clement Clarke Moore, were published that year as a chapter in Foster's book *Author Unknown*. The Livingston descendants may finally have reason to believe the world is "coming around."

The colonial era stone house, where Livingston is said to have recited "A Visit from St. Nicholas" for the first time one Christmas morning circa 1808, was demolished by later owners of the Locust Grove estate.

From a letter sent to Master Timmy Dwight, 7 years old (December 7, 1785)
(Timmy Dwight was the young cousin of Livingston's wife, Sarah)

An Epistle to a Young Friend Just in Breeches

Henry Livingston

Master Timmy brisk and airy
Blythe as Oberon the fairy
On thy head thy cousin wishes
Thousand and ten thousand blisses.

Never may thy wicket ball
In a well or puddle fall;
Or thy wild ambitious kite
O'er the elm's thick foliage light.

When on bended knee thou sittest
And the mark in fancy hittest
May thy marble truly trace
Where thy wishes mark'd the place.

If at hide and seek you play,
All involved in the hay
Titt'ring hear the joyful sound
"Timmy never can be found."

If you hop or if you run
Or whatever is the fun,
Vic'try with her sounding pinion
Hover o'er her little minion.

But when hunger calls the boys
From their helter skelter joys:
Bread and cheese in order standing
For their most rapacious handling
Timmy may thy luncheon be
More than Ben's as five to three.

But if hasty pudding's dish
Meet thy vast capacious wish -
Or lob-lollys charming jelly
Court thy cormorantal belly
Mortal foe to meagre fast
Be thy spoonful first and last.

Written in a 1786 letter to Livingston's brother Beekman (nicknamed "Baze") who was then living in New Lebanon, New York working in the store of his brother-in-law Paul Schneck.

To My Dear Brother Beekman

Henry Livingston

To my dear brother Beekman I sit down to write
Ten minutes past eight and a very cold night.
Not far from me sits with a baullancy cap on
Our very good couzin, Elizabeth Tappen,
A tighter young seamstress you'd ne'er wish to see
New shirts and new cravats this morning cut out
Are tumbled in heaps and lye huddled about.
My wardrobe (a wonder) will soon be enriched
With ruffles new hemmed & wristbands new stitched.
Believe me dear brother tho women may be
Compared to us, of inferiour degree
Yet still they are useful I vow with a fegs
When our shirts are in tatters & jackets in rags.

Now for news my sweet fellow - first learn with a sigh
That matters are carried here gloriously high
Such gadding - such ambling - such jaunting about
To tea with Miss Nancy - to sweet Willy's rout
New parties at coffee - then parties at wine
Next day all the world with the Major must dine
Then bounce all hands to Fishkill must go in a clutter
To guzzle bohea and destroy bread & butter
While you at New Lebanon stand all forlorn
Behind the cold counter from ev'ning to morn
The old tenor merchants push nigher and nigher
Till fairly they shut out poor Baze from the fire.

Out out my dear brother Aunt Amy's just come
With a flask for molasses and a bottle for rum.
Run! help the poor creature to light from her jade
You see the dear lady's a power afraid.
Souse into your arms she leaps like an otter

And smears your new coat with her piggin of butter
Next an army of shakers your quarters beleager
With optics distorted & visages meagre
To fill their black runlets with brandy & gin
Two blessed exorcists to drive away sin.

But laugh away sorrow nor mind it a daisy
Since it matters but little my dear brother Bazee
Whether you are rolling in pastime and pleasure
Or up at New Lebanon taffety measure
If the sweetest of lasses, Contentment, you find
And the banquet enjoy of an undisturb'd mind
   Of friendship and love let who will make a pother
   Believe me dear Baze your affectionate brother
   Will never forget the fifth son of his mother.

p.s. If it suits your convenience remit if you please
To my good brother Paul an embrace & a squeeze.

A Visit from St. Nicholas

Henry Livingston (?)

Twas the night before Christmas, when all thro' the house,
Not a creature was stirring, not even a mouse;
The stockings were hung by the chimney with care,
In hopes that St. Nicholas soon would be there;
The children were nestled all snug in their beds,
While visions of sugar plums danc'd in their heads,
And Mama in her 'kerchief, and I in my cap,
Had just settled our brains for a long winter's nap -
When out on the lawn there arose such a clatter,
I sprang from the bed to see what was the matter.
Away to the window I flew like a flash,
Tore open the shutters, and threw up the sash.
The moon on the breast of the new fallen snow,
Gave the lustre of mid-day to objects below;
When, what to my wondering eyes should appear,
But a miniature sleigh, and eight tiny rein-deer,
With a little old driver, so lively and quick,
I knew in a moment it must be St. Nick.
More rapid than eagles his coursers they came,
And he whistled, and shouted, and call'd them by name:
"Now! Dasher, now! Dancer, now! Prancer, and Vixen,
On! Comet, on! Cupid, on! Dunder and Blixem;
To the top of the porch! to the top of the wall!
Now dash away! dash away! dash away all!"
As dry leaves before the wild hurricane fly,
When they meet with an obstacle, mount to the sky;
So up to the house-top the coursers they flew,
With the sleigh full of Toys - and St. Nicholas too:
And then in a twinkling, I heard on the roof
The prancing and pawing of each little hoof.
As I drew in my head, and was turning around,
Down the chimney St. Nicholas came with a bound:
He was dress'd all in fur, from his head to his foot,
And his clothes were all tarnish'd with ashes and soot;
A bundle of toys was flung on his back,
And he look'd like a peddler just opening his pack:

His eyes - how they twinkled! his dimples how merry,
His cheeks were like roses, his nose like a cherry;
His droll little mouth was drawn up like a bow,
And the beard of his chin was as white as the snow;
The stump of a pipe he held tight in his teeth,
And the smoke it encircled his head like a wreath.
He had a broad face, and a little round belly
That shook when he laugh'd, like a bowl full of jelly:
He was chubby and plump, a right jolly old elf,
And I laugh'd when I saw him in spite of myself;
A wink of his eye and a twist of his head
Soon gave me to know I had nothing to dread.
He spoke not a word, but went straight to his work,
And fill'd all the stockings; then turn'd with a jerk,
And laying his finger aside of his nose
And giving a nod, up the chimney he rose.
He sprung to his sleigh, to his team gave a whistle,
And away they all flew, like the down of a thistle:
But I heard him exclaim, ere he drove out of sight -
Happy Christmas to all, and to all a good night.

(first published anonymously in the Troy Sentinel, *1823)*

William Wilson (1801-1860)

William Wilson left his native Scotland in 1832 and settled in Poughkeepsie at age 31 as a book publisher, seller and binder.

After Wilson's death, his dear friend and colleague, historian Benson Lossing traced the origins of Wilson's picturesque Highland charm to Wilson's impoverished Scottish childhood and romantic mother:

> ...long winter nights when she was toiling at her wheel and distaff, he would sit upon an old counterpane spread for him upon the bare floor of the cottage, near a poor turf fire, without shoes or stockings (for he had none), and read to her from the blessed Book of Life, until his eyelids longed for sleep. Then she would charm him by singing old Scottish ballads, in the lore of which she was deeply versed. She sang the strains of her native land with unusual sweetness and warmth of feeling; and she early imparted to the child a love of music, poetry and romance which gave tone to his intellectual life ever afterward. [1]

As a youth in Scotland, Wilson worked 16 hour days as a Glasgow "lapper" (cloth folder) and later worked as a coal merchant in Edinburgh - all the while writing captivating ballads, poems and prose articles as well as editing literary journals. His fine singing voice and beautiful renditions of old Scottish songs and ballads delighted many in the Scottish literary world.

His life in Poughkeepsie was one of great modesty and relative obscurity. Most of his writing appeared anonymously. Only at the end of his life did he consider collecting his poems and publishing them under his own name. Lossing observed that "only a few knew his real moral and intellectual worth."

The Lily O' Glenlyon

William Wilson

Sweet is the e'eing's tear o'dew
Upon the bending harebell blue,
But sweeter far is she I lo'e, -
   The Lily o' Glenlyon.

I've kissed wi'mony a Highland quean,
Wi' Lowland maids danc'd on the green,
But nane like her I kiss'd yestreen, -
   The Lily o'Glenlyon.

O, thou art sweet as e'ening's gale
That whispers down the blossom'd dale,
An' soft as lover's wooing tale, -
   Sweet Lily o' Glenlyon.

I've seen the rose in lordly bower,
The violet bloom by ruined tower,
But thou art beauty's peerless flower, -
   Sweet Lily o' Glenlyon.

Nae gems thy gouden ringlets braid,
Thy brawest veil's the tartan plaid,
My Highland love, my mountain maid,
   My Lily o' Glenlyon.

Thy rosy cheek, thy deep-blue e'e,
That shot sic deadly glaumerie,
Hath bound my heart for aye to thee,
   Sweet Lily o' Glenlyon.

Scotland

William Wilson

O the bonny hills o' Scotland! I think I see
    them noo,
Wi' robes o' purple heather bloom and rugged
    peaks of blue,
Here mountain glen is ringing wi' shep-
    herd's melodie,
While laverock upward winging is not more
    blithe than he.

O the flowery howns o' Scotland, her haughs
    and gowany braes,
Where blooming, lovesome maidens barefoot
    are bleaching claes,
And gleesome bairns are skirling, and tenty
    carlines scauld,
And rosy health is glowing on cheek o' young
    and auld!

To the bonny streams o' Scotland, her lochs
    and wimplin' burns,
My waking visions wander, my sleeping love
    returns;
And there the birken sheeling to fancy comes
    again,
Wi' Jean at gloamin stealing to meet me i'
    the glen.

O the storied fields of Scotland are fraught
    with battle lore,
They're rife with Roman mem'ries, they're
    rank with Danish gore;
And lion-hearted Wallace wight, the flower of
    chivalrie,
And Bruce of Bannockburn, shall ne'er for-
    gotten be.

O the holy men of Scotland, that muster'd
  in their might
To breast corruption's torrent spate, and battle
  for the right!
Each spot rever'd where freely forth their sa-
  cred lives were given,
Shall ever, like an altar fane, send incense
  sweet to heaven.

O thrice beloved Scotia! my honored mither
  dear,
A wanderer's bosom truly beats for thee from
  year to year;
And when this mortal pilgrimage his weary
  feet hath trod,
He fain would take his final sleep beneath a
  Scottish sod.

Bonnie Mary

William Wilson

When the sun gaes doun, when the sun gaes
   doun,
I'll meet thee, bonnie Mary, when the sun
   gaes doun;
I'll row my apron up, and I'll leave the reeky
   town,
And meet thee by the burnie when the sun
   gaes doun.

By the burnie there's a bower, we will gently
   lean us there,
An' forget in ither's arms every earthly care,
For the chiefest of my joys in this weary
   mortal roun'
Is the burnside wi'Mary, when the sun gaes
   doun.
      When the sun gaes doun.

There's the ruined castle tower on the distant
   steep appears,
Like a hoary auld warrior faded with years;
An the burnie stealin' by wi' a fairy silver
   soun'
Will sooth us wi' its music when the sun
   gaes doun.
      When the sun gaes doun.

The burnie is sweet when the dew is on the
   flower,
But 'tis like a little heaven at the trystin' hour.
An' with pity I would look on the king who
   wears the crown
When wi' thee by the burnie, when the sun
   gaes doun.
      When the sun gaes doun.

When the sun gaes doun, when the sun gaes
    doun,
I'll meet thee by the burnie, when the sun
    gaes down;
Come in thy petticoatie, and thy little drugget
    gown,
An' I'll meet thee, bonnie Mary, when the
    sun gaes doun.

Sweet Lammas Moon

William Wilson

Sweet Lammas moon, thy silvery beam
  Brings many blissful thoughts to me,
Of days when in my first love dream
  I blest thy light on Craigie Lea.

And well I might - for thy young ray
  Ne'er shone on fairer love than mine;
Nor ever youth met maiden gay
  Beneath a brighter gleam than thine.

And well I might - for Mary's charms
  Upon my bosom lay reclined,
While round her slender waist my arms
  In fondest love were closely twined.

And there and then, in that blest hour,
  We plighted vows of changeless faith;
Vows breathed with passion's warmest power
  And broken by the hand of death.

Sweet Lammas moon, then thy young ray
  Shone on my Mary's peerless bloom;
Now waningly, in slow decay,
  Thou beamest coldly on her tomb.

Maria James (1797-1868)

Maria James was the daughter of Welsh immigrants who first came to Dutchess county as laborers in the slate quarries of Clinton. At age 10, she "entered service" to the family of Reverend Freeborn Garretson and his wife Catherine Livingston Garretson at their estate of Wildercliff in Rhinebeck. Years later when asked to describe her intellectual development, she credited the "good speaking and good reading [aloud]" of the Garretsons and their visitors.[1]

By age 17, she was already a poet although she shrank from the label as "the height of presumption." After working briefly as a mantilla maker and then for several years as a nursemaid, Maria James returned to the employ of the Garretsons of Rhinebeck.

Her poems were composed in her head while doing routine household chores - and only later committed to paper, sometimes weeks after their creation. When once a lady commented, "I suppose your poetry often keeps you awake," James replied: "No, it never kept me awake an hour; but it is often busy with me at the wash-tub - though white-washing is the most favorable." Upon learning that skeptics had questioned whether a "mere" servant could really have written such poems without "help," she responded with the impassioned poem, "What is Poetry?"[2]

In 1839, Maria James' poems were published in the collection *Wales and Other Poems* with an introduction by her literary champion, Bishop Alonzo Potter. For Potter, James' poetic gift was one more proof that "... in every age, God has been raising up one after another from the ranks of menial employment, to shine as lights in the world."[3] After her poems were published, Maria James remained "in service" at Wildercliff for the remaining 29 years of her life.

Photo: Wildercliff (Historic American Buildings Survey)

What is Poetry?

Maria James

A LAMBENT flame within the breast;
A thought harmoniously express'd;
A distant meteor's glimmering ray;
A light that often leads astray;
A harp, whose ever-varying tone
Might waken to the breeze's moan
A lake, in whose transparent face
Fair nature's lovely form we trace;
A blooming flower, in gardens rare,
Yet found in deserts bleak and bare;
A charm o'er every object thrown;
A bright creation of its own;
A burst of feeling, warm and wild,
From nature's own impassion'd child.

The Whip-Poor-Will

Maria James

The ring-dove's note, in eastern climes,
May wing with speed the sultry hours,
And England's boasted nightingale
May charm with song her native bowers; -

Yet there is one, and only one,
Whose note is dearer far to me;
Though his is not the gorgeous plume,
Nor his the voice of harmony.

He shuns the crowded haunts of men,
And hies to forests far away, -
Or seeks some deep, secluded vale,
To pour his solitary lay, -

Or haply at some cottage door,
At fall of night, when all is still,
The rustic inmates pause to hear
The gentle cry of 'Whip-poor-will.'

Sheep-Sorrel

Maria James

There is a flower unknown to fame,
Whose very name is scarce a name,
Which never yet has won its way
To lady's bower or minstrel's lay.

No product this of sweat and toil, -
Growth of no rich luxuriant soil;
The common hillocks, brown and bare, -
You need but look, to find it there.

Five petals small of palest gold,
The early smiles of spring unfold;
Nor has its glory pass'd away
On chill November's latest day.

Light pois'd upon its stem is seen
A curious leaf of tender green -
Three hearts distinct, yet bound together,
Alike in storm and sunny weather.

Oh, Nature! what a book is thine!
Through every page we read divine,
Calling the simplest weed to prove
How brothers, sisters, friends should love.

The Broom

Maria James

Give me a broom, one neatly made
In Niscayuna's distant shade;
Or bearing full its staff upon
The well-known impress, 'Lebanon.'
A handle slender, smooth, and light,
Of bass-wood, or of cedar white;
Where softest palm from point to heel
Might ne'er a grain of roughness feel -
So firm, a fix, the stalks confine;
So tightly drawn the hempen line;
Then fan-like spread divided wove,
As fingers in a lady's glove -
To crown the whole, (and save beside,)
The loop, the buckskin loop is tied.

With this in hand, small need to care
If C.....y or J.......n fill the chair -
What in the banks is said or done -
The game at Texas lost or won -
How city belles collect their rings,
And hie to Saratoga springs; -
To Erie's, or Ontarios's shore,
To hear Niagara's thunders roar -
While undisturb'd my course I keep,
Cheer'd by the sound of sweep, sweep, sweep.

See learned Doctors rack their brains,
To cure mankind of aches and pains,
When half, and more than half, arise
From want of prudence, - exercise.
The body like a garment wears,
And aches and pains may follow years;
But when I see the young, the gay,
Untimely droop, and pine away,
As if the life of life were o'er,

Each day less active than before, -
Their courage fled, their interest cold, -
With firmer grasp, my broom I hold.
Nor is this all; in very deed
The broom may prove a friend in need;
On this I lean, - on this depend;
With such a surety, such a friend,
There's not a merchant in the place
Who would refuse me silk or lace;
Or linen-fine, or broad-cloth dear,
Or e'en a shawl of fam'd Cashmere,
Though prudence whispering, still would say,
"Remember, there's a rainy day."

Hand me the broom, (a matron said,)
As down the hose and ball were laid;
I think your father soon will come;
I long to see him safe at home.
Pile on the wood, and set the chair, -
The supper and the board prepare;
The gloom of night is gathering fast, -
The storm is howling o'er the waste.

The hearth is swept, arrang'd the room
And duly hung the shaker-broom,
While cheerful smiles and greetings wait
The master entering at his gate.
Let patriots, poets, twine their brows
With laurel, or with holly boughs;
But let the broom-corn wreath be mine,
Adorn'd with many a sprig of pine;
With wild-flowers from the forest deep,
And garlands from the craggy steep,
Which ne'er have known the gardener's care,
But rise, and bloom spontaneous there.

Fitz-Greene Halleck *(1790-1867)*

Few have ever heard of the 19th century poet who gives Poets' Walk Park its name. Even fewer are familiar with his work. Poet Fitz-Greene Halleck had only a ten year period of productivity (from 1817 to 1827) before sinking into forty years of silence. The scant body of work he did complete was of decidedly uneven quality.

Yet in the first half of the 19th century, Halleck was enormously popular with the general public and highly respected by his literary colleagues. Oliver Wendell Holmes and John Greenleaf Whittier wrote poetic tributes in memory of Halleck, and during his life, Edgar Allan Poe, Washington Irving, James Fenimore Cooper, and William Cullen Bryant all were among his friends and professional admirers.

In 1877, ten years after his death, 10,000 spectators watched no less than the President of the United States unveil a statue of Halleck on Central Park's "Literary Walk." The *New York Tribune* gushed, "Today, for the first time, an American author will receive the honor of a commemorative statue. Busts, shafts or tablets have been erected to others of the guild of letters. But Fitz-Greene Halleck is the first to be monumentally treated as the equal of statesmen, divines and inventors..."[1]

So who was Fitz-Greene Halleck?

At age 18, Halleck left his native Guilford, Connecticut and moved to New York where he began a prosaic if steady career as a bank clerk. Ten years later, he burst on to the literary stage in 1819 when he found his muse: the brilliant young doctor and poet, Joseph Rodman Drake. Together, they succeeded in convincing the *New York Evening Post* to publish their anonymous comic satires of the city's elite in a display of frothy wit and poetic skill which many had thought impossible in the uncultured world of pioneer America.

Under the pen names of "Croaker" and "Croaker Jr.," Drake and Halleck became literary sensations, although Halleck later dismissed the Croaker poems as "harmless pleasantries" of transitory interest. The poems' frequent and now obscure allusions to events, people and places of early

New York make them largely impenetrable to modern readers; but their fine melodic flow and bubbly joie de vivre are still readily felt even today.

When Halleck's beloved friend and partner Drake died at age 25, Halleck wrote an elegy of such power and simple beauty that it instantly entered the ranks of "most quoted poems" and remains the only poem for which Halleck is noted today.

After Drake's death, Halleck went on to write a few other poems of consequence - particularly the stirring blood and thunder poem "Marco Bozzaris" - a once commonly anthologized verse that was memorized and recited by countless school children even into the early 20th century.

As a person, Halleck was a remarkable blend of disciplined accountant and graceful bonvivant. For 17 years, he wrote virtually nothing while acting as the private secretary and personal companion of America's richest man, John Jacob Astor. From 8am to 2pm, he managed Astor's business affairs, while his evenings were often spent entertaining Astor's literary social circle with his renowned gift for quick repartee and sparkling humor.

One of his most celebrated witticisms was his description of meeting the famously silent author Nathaniel Hawthorne: "We happened to sit together, and I assure you that for an hour we talked almost incessantly, although Hawthorne said nothing."[2]

In his private hours, he could be seen prowling the City's streets - usually at night, muttering the poems he would create in his head while rhythmically swinging time with his trademark green umbrella. Occasionally, Halleck took short breaks in Dutchess County at Rokeby, the Red Hook estate of Astor's son, William Backhouse Astor. Poets' Walk Park, formerly part of Rokeby, evokes the pastoral landscape paths that Halleck would have strolled - along with another favorite guest of the Astors, writer Washington Irving.[3]

When John Jacob Astor died in 1848, with a fortune of twenty million dollars, he left only $200 a year to Halleck. Friends thought this Astor's posthumous rebuttal to a comment Halleck had once made to Astor: "Of what use is all this money to you? I would be content to live upon a couple of hundreds a year for the rest of my life."

Always the impeccable courtly gentleman, Halleck responded to the news of his paltry inheritance with gratitude rather than rancor. Astor's son, however, seemed to feel the injustice and contributed an additional $10,000 to Halleck's final settlement.[4]

Halleck's remaining years were spent with his unmarried sister, living an isolated life in his provincial Connecticut hometown in apparent retreat from the Civil War America he held in utter contempt. In earlier times, however, his poetic gifts had given Americans their first thrilling sense of cultural pride and the confidence to believe that their country could produce a sophisticated poetic voice.

Today, every year on Halleck's birthday, members of the tongue in cheek "Fitz-Greene Halleck Society" gather at Halleck's Central Park statue near 67th Street to share rejection letters and "commemorate the fickle nature of fame."[5] As they point up at the bronze statue of Halleck next to statues of Shakespeare, Sir Walter Scott and Roberts Burns, they ask passersby hopefully, "Would you like to learn about America's first great poet?" Most reply, "No, thanks."

On the Death of Joseph Rodman Drake

Fitz-Greene Halleck

Green be the turf above thee,
  Friend of my better days!
None knew thee but to love thee,
  Nor named thee but to praise.

Tears fell when thou wert dying,
  From eyes unused to weep,
And long, where thou art lying,
  Will tears the cold turf steep.

When hearts, whose truth was proven,
  Like thine, are laid in earth,
There should a wreath be woven
  To tell the world their worth;

And I who woke each morrow
  To clasp thy hand in mine,
Who shared thy joy and sorrow,
  Whose weal and woe were thine;

It should be mine to braid it
  Around thy faded brow;
But I've in vain essayed it,
  And feel I cannot now.

While memory bids me weep thee,
  Nor thoughts nor words are free, -
The grief is fixed too deeply
  That mourns a man like thee.

Cutting

Fitz-Greene Halleck

The world is not a perfect one,
    All women are not wise or pretty,
All that are willing are not won -
    More's the pity - more's the pity!
"Playing Wall-flower's rather flat,"
    L'Allegro or Penseroso -
Not that women care for that -
    But oh! they hate the slighting beau so!

Delia says my dancing's bad -
    She's found it out since I have cut her;
She says wit I never had -
    I said she "smelt of bread and butter."
Mrs. Milton coldly bows -
    I did not think her baby "cunning."
Gertrude says I've little "Nous" -
    I tired of her atrocious punning.

Tom's wife says my taste is vile -
    I condemned her macarony;
Miss McLush, my flirt awhile,
    Hates me - I preferred her crony;
Isabella, Sarah Anne,
    Fat Estella, and one other,
Call me an immoral man -
    I have cut their drinking brother.

Thus it is - be only civil -
    Dance with stupid, short and tall -
Know no line 'twixt saint and devil -
    Spend your wit on fools and all -
Simper with the milk-and-waters -
    Suffer bores, and talk of caps -
Trot out people's awkward daughters -
    You may scandal 'scape - perhaps!

But prefer the wise and pretty -

Pass Reserve to dance with Wit -
Let the slight be e'er so petty,
    Pride will never pardon it.
Woman never yet refused
    Virtues to a seeming wooer -
Woman never yet abused
    Him who had been civil to her.

Marco Bozzaris

Fitz-Greene Halleck

At midnight, in his guarded tent,
   The Turk was dreaming of the hour
When Greece, her knee in suppliance bent,
   Should tremble at his power:
In dreams, through camp and court, he bore
The trophies of a conqueror;
  In dreams his song of triumph heard;
Then wore his monarch's signet ring:
Then pressed that monarch's throne - a king;
As wild his thoughts, and gay of wing,
   As Eden's garden bird.

At midnight, in the forest shades,
   Bozzaris ranged his Suliote band,
True as the steel of their tried blades,
   Heroes in heart and hand.
There had the Persian's thousands stood,
There had the glad earth drunk their blood
   On old Plataea's day;
And now there breathed that haunted air
The sons of sires who conquered there,
With arm to strike and soul to dare,
   As quick, as far as they.

An hour passed on - the Turk awoke;
   That bright dream was his last;
He woke - to hear his sentries shriek,
"To arms! they come! the Greek! the Greek!"
He woke - to die midst flame, and smoke,
And shout, and groan, and saber stroke,
   And death shots falling thick and fast
As lightnings from the mountain cloud;
And heard, with voice as trumpet loud,
   Bozzaris cheer his band:
"Strike - till the last armed foe expires;
Strike - for your altars and your fires;

Strike - for the green graves of your sires;
   God - and your native land!"

They fought - like brave men, long and well;
   They piled that ground with Moslem slain,
They conquered - but Bozzaris fell,
   Bleeding at every vein.
His few surviving comrades saw
His smile when rang their proud hurrah,
   And the red field was won;
Then saw in death his eyelids close
Calmly, as to a night's repose,
   Like flowers at set of sun.

Come to the bridal-chamber, Death!
   Come to the mother's, when she feels
For the first time, her first-born's breath;
   Come when the blessed seals
That close the pestilence are broke;
And crowded cities wail its stroke;
Come in consumption's ghastly form,
The earthquake shock, the ocean storm;
Come when the heart beats high and warm
   With banquet song, and dance, and wine;
And thou art terrible - the tear,
The groan, the knell, the pall, the bier,
And all we know, or dream, or fear
   Of agony, are thine.

But to the hero, when his sword
   Has won the battle for the free;
Thy voice sounds like a prophet's word;
And in its hollow tones are heard
   The thanks of millions yet to be.
Come, when his task of fame is wrought -
Come, with her laurel leaf, blood-bought -
   Come in her crowning hour - and then
Thy sunken eye's unearthly light
To him is welcome as the sight
   Of sky and stars to prisoned men;
Thy grasp is welcome as the hand

Of brother in a foreign land;
Thy summons welcome as the cry
That told the Indian isles were nigh
    To the world-seeking Genoese,
When the land wind, from woods of palm,
And orange groves, and fields of balm,
    Blew o'er the Haytian seas.

Bozzaris! with the storied brave
    Greece nurtured in her glory's time,
Rest thee - there is no prouder grave,
    Even in her own proud clime.
She wore no funeral weeds for thee,
    Nor bade the dark hearse wave its plume
Like torn branch from death's leafless tree
In sorrow's pomp and pageantry,
    The heartless luxury of the tomb;
But she remembers thee as one
Long loved and for a season gone;
For thee her poet's lyre is wreathed,
Her marble wrought, her music breathed;
For thee she rings the birthday bells;
Of thee her babe's first lisping tells;
For thine her evening prayer is said
At palace couch and cottage bed;
Her soldier, closing with the foe,
Gives for thy sake a deadlier blow;
His plighted maiden, when she fears
For him the joy of her young years,
Thinks of thy fate, and checks her tears;
    And she, the mother of thy boys,
Though in her eye and faded cheek
Is read the grief she will not speak,
    The memory of her buried joys,
And even she who gave thee birth,
Will, by their pilgrim-circled hearth,
    Talk of thy doom without a sigh;
For thou art Freedom's now, and Fame's:
One of the few, the immortal names,
    That were not born to die.

Rokeby

When Margaret Rebecca Astor chose the name "Rokeby" for her family's country seat in Barrytown, little could she have known how well she had chosen. While reading Sir Walter Scott's 1813 poem "Rokeby," Mrs. Astor was particularly struck by one wildly romantic passage describing a woodland glen so much like her own "Devil's Gorge" along the Mudder Kill, that she persuaded her father, General John Armstrong, to rename the property "Rokeby." [1]

The dramatic, tempestuous and altogether stunning splendor of Sir Walter Scott's Rokeby glen has indeed been an apt symbol for the fascinating and by now well known family saga of Margaret Astor's descendants, the famous "Astor orphans." The estate's original name, La Bergerie (The Sheepfold), would have been an ironic name indeed in a family so noted for its individuality.

From *Rokeby, Canto II:*
(the poem's stream, "Greta" reminded Mrs. Astor of the "Mudder Kill")

...The open vale is soon past o'er,
Rokeby, though nigh, is seen no more;
Sinking mid Greta's thickets deep,
A wild and darker course they keep,
A stern and lone, yet lovely road,
As e'er the foot of Minstrel trode!
Broad shadows o'er their passage fell,
Deeper and narrower grew the dell;
It seemed some mountain, rent and riven,
A channel for the stream had given,
So high the cliffs of limestone grey
Hung beetling o'er the torrent's way,
Yielding, along their rugged base,

A flinty footpath's niggard space,
 Where he, who winds 'twixt rock and wave,
May hear the headlong torrent wave,
And like a steed in frantic fit,
That flings the froth from curb and bit,
May view her chafe her waves to spray,
O'er every rock that bars her way,
Till foam-globes on her eddies ride,
Thick as the schemes of human pride,
That down life's current drive amain
As frail as frothy and as vain!

The cliffs, that rear the haughty head
High o'er the river's darksome bed,
Were now all naked, wild, and grey,
Now waving all with greenwood spray;
Here trees to every crevice clung,
And o'er the dell their branches hung;
And there, all splintered and uneven,
The shivered rocks ascend to heaven;
Oft, too, the ivy swathed their breast,
And wreathed its garland round their crest,
Or from the spires bade loosely flare
Its tendrils in the middle air.
As pennons wont to wave of old
O'er the high feast of Baron bold,
When revelled loud the feudal rout,
And the arched halls returned their shout,
Such and more wild is Greta's roar,
And such the echoes from her shore,
And so the ivied banners gleam,
Waved wildly o'er the brawling stream...

Springside

In 1850, a small 44 acre farm on the outskirts of Poughkeepsie captured the attention of wealthy local brewer Matthew Vassar. Vassar's biographer, Benson Lossing described the farm as being in a state of "natural rudeness" when Vassar first saw it: "Wooded knolls arose above tangled hollows. Springs gushed out from oozy little hillsides...The domain was unattractive, idle wild." [1]

But in the farm's curious rocky knolls, winding rivulets and bubbling springs, Vassar recognized an intriguing topography and purchased it for use as a new public cemetery. Poughkeepsie's citizens had other ideas, however, and the cemetery was eventually located a mile away along the Hudson River.

Undaunted, Vassar decided to make the farm into his own country seat and hired America's most celebrated tastemaker, Newburgh's Andrew Jackson Downing to design the estate's buildings and grounds. As the last documented Downing landscape still surviving in America, Springside remains a symbol of Downing's influential ideas and brilliant talent for creating landscapes of power and artistry.

For many years, the public was allowed to stroll the Springside grounds, where each scenic feature had been fondly named by Vassar himself. Downing's ability to transform a "rude" farm into a dazzling landscape evoked the following poetic tribute from a visitor awed by the transformation.

For the Poughkeepsie Eagle *(June 7, 1852)*
"Lines written impromptu, by a visitor to the gounds of M. Vassar Esq.,
he having often (while in the barren state) rambulated over them while
in his boyhood."

Ode to Springside

Oh tell me not that Paradise
   Bloomed in the distant East,
Ere culture o'er this darkened world
   Her radiant light had cast.

No; Paradise near him is found,
   As future poets will sing,
And nature's beauties ever crown
   "Springside's" returning spring.

The old Dutch barn and farmhouse gone,
   Wild grasses, bogs and thistles,
The untilled hills and barren knolls
   Now yield their golden fleeces.

Sour grew the rough and stunted fruit,
   Within the wild, full bough
But now amidst the pruned limbs,
   Delicious fruit doth grow.

Where the stagnant pools and miry sloughs
   With croaking frogs all over;
The willow larch, and myrtle grows
   Like pigs in luxuriant clover.

The gardener's cottage dimly seen
   In distance, thro' the wood,
The rural lawns and evergreens
   Replace the wild abode.

The clustered pile of farm-yard steads
   With artistic skill arranged,

Tho' last, are not the least to claim
   Our admiration's praise.

Thus in the future, brighter years,
   Progression's laws provide,
Unfolding still, with newer charms,
   Fresh beauties of "Springside."

Then glowing hope with heavenly fruits
   Shall cheer our labors on,
Till this once dreamy barren waste,
   "Springside" we'll call "sweet home."

Founder's Day

In 1866, Vassar College began a tradition of setting aside one day in the academic year to commemorate the beneficence and wisdom of Matthew Vassar.

The first "Founder's Day" (on Vassar's birthday of April 29th) began with a surprise reception. As Vassar's carriage turned in at the main college gate, 300 students lined the entrance drive smiling and waving white handkerchiefs. Vassar was moved to tears.

Following the welcome ceremony, students presented a "literary exercise" of essays, songs and poetry written for the occasion. Vassar sat in the college chapel with the students he called his "college children" and heard for the first time the poem "Hilltop Idyl" by Miss Sarah L. Stilson of Nunda, New York.

Later, Vassar reread Stilson's poem, calling it "a beautiful little gem composition" and ordered a printing of 200 copies. Vassar kept 25 copies to distribute among his friends and continued a friendly correspondence with Stilson until his death two years later.[1]

(In Stilson's poem, Vassar girls encounter a strange, prophesizing spirit while watching the sun rise on Founder's Day morning. Although the spirit is concerned that the girls will be late for the breakfast bell and their rehearsals for the Founder's Day program, he pauses to offer them both stern warnings and inspiring predictions for the future of Vassar College.)

Illustration: Bust of Matthew Vassar

Hilltop Idyl

Sarah L. Stilson

Dawn kissed the Catskills, whose calm face smiled
    Blushing back on Dawn,
So, beauty-bathed, the jealous stars had one by one
    withdrawn;
A band of girls on "Sunset Hill' watched for the
    coming day,
They tho't they heard a far strange sound, and then
    a still voice say: -

"I'm Guardian Genius of the place. Look! where
    yon College stands,
Five years ago no structure vast showed work of
    builders' hands;
The herdsman's whistle might be heard, or cattle's
    distant low:
A great mind's Thought begets a Deed, - what greets
    the vision now?
One philanthropic soul was stirred to elevate your
    race,
To open Wisdom's gates to give Columbia's daughters
    place.
Men praised the work: its Founder said, 'Give me
    not now the praise -
'Tis but a soulless form as yet - 'twill speak in future
    days.'
They gathered in from distant homes, from cities scat-
    tered wide,
Where rice fields wave, where north winds sweep
    where west streams roll their tide,
Until the structure woke to life. Lights from the win-
    dows gleamed;
With voices rang the corridors that with earnest young
    life teemed;
And still, 'Not yet,' the Founder said, - 'when
    women you shall see
Go forth to bless when I am gone, then shall my tri-

umph be.'...

But he has passed life's rapids, lo! their foam is on his
hair,

And the blinding spray has dimmed his eye from the
sea that draweth near.

What you should write, I scarce can tell: your daily
influence preaches

Far louder sermons day by day than all your silvery
speeches.

Talk not on 'Woman's Rights:' Be right, and leave
the praise to men.

But hark! the corridor breakfast bells are ringing out
again.

On those disheveled locks all eyes' reproving glance
will fall,

If tardy, or with lingering steps you thread that din-
ing-hall:

'Twere poetry on Sunset Hill to watch day's rosy flash,

But poetry and prose in life do sometimes sadly clash.

So hence, as you must practice o'er today the 'Found-
er's Greeting:'"

"Or, more important," added one, "attend committee
meeting.

Nay Guardian Spirit, 'tis but dawn, 'twas only rising
bell,

Phoebus has not joined his steeds above the gold-
crowned hill,

So of this College phophesy the future destiny."

"Students, the answer yours," it said; "'tis left for
you to say:

'Tis a grand interrogation-point before the world to-
day;

And so, 'to be or not to be, that is the question' then,

Whether you'll rise in mental height to regions most
divine,

Or, leaving Minerva's temple gates, offer on Fashion's
shrine.

If the last, your verdict then will be - your verdict
and the world's

That Curtiss' 'goddesses,' alas! are only common

                    girls.
You'll wander forth from the Founder's halls, but
    each one of your band,
Tho' little, keeps (O sacred trust!) his honor in her
    hand.
Live not for self; live for your age, the future, and to
    God;
Thus each a gem in his shining crown, when he sleeps
    beneath the sod.
Despise no humble mission, overlooking lowly worth,
The bow that crowns the heaven begins and ends its
    arch on earth.
Toil on! up Wisdom's starry heights, faint not in as-
    piration;
Your best achievement will be but his life-dream's
    incarnation,
And Vassar College stand thro' time an honor to the
    Nation."

Illustration: Vassar College Main Building
(Special Collections, Vassar College Libraries)

Myron Benton (1834-1902)

Poet, scholar and farmer Myron Benton was the third generation owner of Amenia's celebrated 800 acre estate "Troutbeck" - named after the English Lake District village associated with Benton's favorite poet, Samuel Taylor Coleridge.

Although known today largely as the close friend of naturalist John Burroughs and the recipient of Henry Thoreau's last letter, Benton's poems are small, quiet treasures deeply reflective of his beloved Webutuck Valley. To his friend Burroughs, Benton once explained, "We have hugged the soil close - an unbroken line of farmers; how far back in England green and old I do not know, but doubtless a long way. This bucolic association has permeated the very blood; I feel it in every heartbeat. My intense local attachment I doubt not has been fostered through many generations."[1]

Throughout his life, Benton frequently wrote appreciative notes to other men of letters, and in this way, began his important friendship with John Burroughs. They first met in person in Poughkeepsie in 1862 where they ended their walk through town at Kaal Rock. "We sat there an hour or more and opened our minds to each other," wrote Burroughs. Later they would excitedly pour over their first copy of Whitman's "Leaves of Grass" on a hike through the pastures of Troutbeck. [2]

Benton's poems (which Burroughs compared to "the flavor of sweet cream") appeared in magazines and anthologies and were eventually collected in a volume called *Songs of the Webutuck*. Although his admirers were perplexed by Benton's shy disinterest in more forcefully promoting his work, it was Burroughs who pointed out that Benton's concept of poetry extended beyond mere words:

> Mr. Benton is a poet who writes his poetry in the landscape as well as in books...Planter of trees and vines, preserver of old picturesque cottages, lover of paths and streams, beautifier of highways, friend of all wild and shy things, historian and portrayer of big trees, collector of local relics and seeker and cultivator of all that gives flavor and character to a place, Mr. Benton is the practical poet of whom the country everywhere needs many more. [3]

Midsummer Invitation

Myron Benton

O pallid student! leave thy dim alcove
  And stretch one restful summer afternoon,
Thoughtless amidst the thoughtless things of June,
Beneath these boughs with light and murmur wove.

Drop book and pen, a thrall released rove;
      The Sisyphean task flung off, impugn
      The withered Sphynx - with earth's fresh heart attune.
Thou, man, the origin of evil prove!
O leave that dark coil where the spider delves
  To trap the unwary reasoner in his lair,
And weave oblivion's veils round learned shelves;
Wist to the beat of Ariel's happy wings,
  And cool thy brain in this balm laden air;
Here brooding peace shall still thy questionings.

(At Benton's request, this poem was read at his funeral.)

There Is One Spot For Which My Soul Will Yearn

Myron Benton

There is one spot for which my soul will yearn,
May it but come where breeze and sunlight play,
And leaves are glad, some path of swift return;
A waif - a presence borne on friendly ray -
Even thus, if but beneath the same blue sky!
The grazing kine not then will see me cross
The pasture slope; the swallows will not shy,
Nor brooding thrush; blithe bees the flowers will
   toss:
Not the faint thistle down *my* breath may charm.
Ah, me! But I shall find the dear ways old,
If I have to leave, that sheltered valley farm;
Its climbing woods, its spring, the meadow's gold;
   The creek-path, dearest to my boyhood's feet -
   Oh God! is there another world so sweet?

The Mowers

Myron Benton

The sunburnt mowers are in the swath -
    Swing, swing, swing!
  The towering lilies loath
   Tremble and totter and fall;
    The meadow-rue
Dashes its tassels of golden dew;
   And the keen blade sweeps o'er all -
    Swing, swing, swing!

The flowers, the berries, the feathered grass
   Are thrown in a smothered mass;
Hastens away the butterfly;
With half their burden the brown bees hie;
And the meadow-lark shrieks distrest
And leaves the poor younglings all in the nest.
   The daisies clasp and fall;
And totters the Jacob's ladder tall.
Weaving and winding and curving lithe,
O'er plumy hillocks - through dewy hollows;
     His subtle scythe
   The nodding mower follows-
    Swing, swing, swing!

Anon the chiming hetstones ring -
    Ting-a-ling! Ting-a ling!
     And the mower now
Pauses and wipes his beaded brow.
A moment he scans the fleckless sky;
A moment, the fish-hawk soaring high;
And watches the swallows dip and dive
     Anear and far.
They whisk and glimmer, and chatter and strive;
   What do they gossip together?
     Cunning fellows they are,
     Wise prophets to him!
"Higher or lower they circle and skim -

Fair or foul tomorrow's hay-weather!"

Tallest primroses, or loftiest daisies,
    Not a steel-blue feather
    Of slim wing grazes:
"Fear not! fear not!" cry the swallows.
Each mower tightens his snath-ring's wedge,
    And his finger daintily follows
    The long blade's tickle edge;
Softly the whetstone's last touches ring-
    Ting-a-ling! ting-a-ling!
Like a leaf muffled bird in the woodland nigh,
Faintly the fading echoes reply -
    Ting-a-ling! ting-a-ling!

"Perchance the swallows, that flit in their glee,
Of tomorrow's hay weather know little as we!"
Says Farmer Russet: "Be it hidden in shower
Or sunshine, tomorrow we do not own -
    Today is ours alone!
Not a twinkle we'll waste of the golden hour.
Grasp tightly the nibs - give heel and give toe!
Lay a goodly swath, shaved smooth and low
    Prime is the day -
    Swing, swing, swing!"

Farmer Russet is aged and gray -
Gray as the frost, but fresh as the spring.
    Straight is he
    As the green fir-tree;
And with heart most blithe, and sinews lithe,
He leads the row with his merry scythe.
    "Come boys! strike up the old song
    While we circle around -
The song we always in haytime sing -
    And let the woods ring,
    And let the echoes prolong
    The merry sound!"

(SONG) July is just in the nick of time!
    (Hay-weather, hay-weather;)

The midsummer month is the golden prime
For haycocks smelling of clover and thyme; -
   (Swing all together!)
July is just in the nick of time!

Chorus:
O, we'll make our hay while the good sun shines,
   We'll waste not a golden minute!
No shadow of storm the blue arch lines;
    We'll waste not a minute - not a minute!
      For the west-wind is fair;
       O, the hay-day is rare!
The sky is without a brown cloud in it!

June is too early for richest hay;
   (Fair weather, fair weather;)
The corn stretches taller the livelong day;
But grass is ever too sappy to lay;
   (Clip all together!)
June is too early for richest hay.

August's a month that too far goes by;
   (Late weather, late weather;)
Grasshoppers are chipper and kick too high!
And grass that's standing is fodder scorched dry;
   (Pull all together!)
August's a month that too far goes by.

July is just in the nick of time!
      (Best weather, best weather;)
The midsummer month is the golden prime
For haycocks smelling of clover and thyme;
   (Strike all together!)
July is just in the nick of time!

   Still hiss the scythes;
Shudder the grasses' defenceless blades -
   The lily-throng writhes;
And, as a phalanx of wild-geese streams,
Where the shore of April's cloudland gleams,
On their dizzy way, in serried grades -

Wing on wing, wing on wing -
The mowers, each a step in advance
Of his fellow, time their stroke with a glance
    Of swerveless force;
And far through the meadow leads their course,
    Swing, swing, swing!

Rumination

Myron Benton

O, foolish Brooklet! You have strayed this morning
Into this shade without a courteous warning,
Out of that sleepy swamp, just o'er the hill,
To break your shallow gossip here at will;
Of sluggish life beneath the hardhack bushes,
Amongst the cat-tail flags and waving rushes;
Flirtations of the dragon-flies; the frogs'
Gruff lamentations under toppling bogs;
Of tipsy, reeling snipes, who cannot keep
Their balance midst the osier tangles deep;
Of turtles lifting up their muddy noses
Beneath the buckthorn bloom and gay swamp roses.
And this low life upon the weedy peat
Is all the world to you in young conceit,
My little brook, and nothing old or new
Is half so deep and worldly-wise as you.
And so this leaf-wove shade your prattling noise
Of gossip fills, and drowns the oriole's voice;
But moveth not that wise and ancient cow,
Who chews her juicy cud so languid now
Beneath her favorite elm, whose drooping bough
Lulls all but inward vision fast asleep;
But still her tireless tail, a pendulum-sweep,
Mysterious clock-work guides, and some hid pulley
Her drowsy cud each moment raises duly.
Of this great wondrous world has she seen more
Than you, my little brook, and cropped its store
Of succulent grass on many a mead and lawn,
And strayed to distant uplands in the dawn.
And she has had some dark experience
Of graceless man's ingratitude; and hence
Her ways have not been ways of pleasantness,
Nor all her paths of peace. But her distress
And grief she has lived past; your giddy round
Disturbs her not, for she is learned profound
In deep Brahminical philosophy.
She chews the cud of sweetest revery,
Above your worldly prattle, brooklet merry,
Oblivious of all things sublunary.

Joel Benton *(1832-1911)*

Like his cousin Myron, Joel Benton was a poet and literary scholar who made his home on the grounds of the family's Trout-beck estate in Amenia. But unlike his retiring cousin who was content to write small, exquisite poems along the banks of the Webutuck, Joel Benton sought a more active engagement in civic and cultural life.

At 19, he became the editor of the *Amenia Times* and later served as Amenia's town supervisor. Frustrated with slogging over 30 miles of rough country roads to attend lectures at the county seat, Benton resolved to create his own Lyceum series right in Amenia. He later remarked of this decision, "Mohammed could not make the mountain come to him. I resolved to do better than Mohammed. I would make the mountainous celebrities come to me." [1]

For ten winters, Benton's Lyceum series attracted the leading lecturers of the day, and eager audiences poured in regardless of February snowstorms and the mud of March. Because of this unusually lively intellectual ferment, Amenia became known as a Dutchess County version of Concord, Massachusetts.

Benton's large acquaintance with the celebrities of his era provided many entertaining anecdotes that he later turned into published accounts. In one reminiscence from his Lyceum days, Benton recalled how Mark Twain had once pulled him aside just before stepping on stage with a rather odd request not to be introduced to the audience. A puzzled Benton agreed to cooperate. Once out on stage, Twain sat silently while the audience (and Benton!) grew increasingly uncomfortable.

After several awkward moments, Twain finally rose and said, "Ladies and Gentlemen: I have lectured many years and in many towns, large and small. I have travelled north, south, east, and west. I have met many great men: very great men. But I have never yet in all my travels met the president of a country lyceum who could introduce me to an audience with the distinguished consideration which my merits deserve." The audience roared.[2]

As a scholar, Benton's great passion was the work of Ralph Waldo Emerson. But it is his description of attending Emerson's 1852 lecture in Poughkeepsie that is most remarkable. If Benton is remembered at all today, it is less for his scholarship and poetry than for his fascinating encounters with 19th century celebrities.

Of his visit to Poughkeepsie to hear Emerson, Benton wrote:

> I set out with a friend, both of us then young men - to drive 20 miles on wheels over rough winter roads...We had both read his book, and were more aroused to listen to his voice and take account of his looks than we should have been to see the President of the United States...

> A full audience was assembled in the public hall when the lecture hour arrived, and it was typical of all classes. Only a small fraction of it, however, was much acquainted with the lecturer's work, though few probably were ignorant of his reputation...His voice was singularly mellow and modulated - put forth as if the thoughts uttered were just being born, and not already on paper - and punctuated by steady halts and an emphasis that were themselves helpful and charming...

> But there were various and bewildered comments upon the lecture, when the audience walked out, in spite of the rapt and silent attention that had been given to it. With many there seemed to be a sense of something that had been shot over their heads, and hit a mark they could not or did not see.

> I should have said his manuscript was a mass of loose leaves, like a pack of cards, and apparently they sometimes got intermixed, causing an occasional momentary pause to look the right one up. But it used to be said that even this added a thrill to the lecture - perhaps because you could linger a little yourself, during the silence, to ponder upon what has just been spoken.

> Some said it made no difference if he picked up the wrong leaf, or shuffled them as if they actually were a pack of cards. As the continuity of thought was a spiritual one, rather than one of syntax or of logic, the brilliant intuitions went equally well in any order... [3]

The following is an example of Benton's "public occasion poetry" delivered at Pough-keepsie's Collingwood Opera House in 1888 on the 100th anniversary of New York State's ratification of the Constitution.

In dramatic debates at the Poughkeepsie courthouse during the long hot summer of 1788, New York's delegates had moved the young nation toward a strong federal system of government balanced by the protection of individual and states rights. One hundred years later in 1888, thousands came to Poughkeepsie to celebrate this historic anniversary with a huge parade, a "civic exercise" at the Opera House (where Benton recited his poem) and a grand fireworks display over the Poughkeepsie Railroad Bridge.

Poem

Joel Benton

Here met, a hundred years ago,
  Men of rare stature, stern, sedate,
Who by the Hudson's lordly flow,
  Sat, arbiters of law and fate.

The cannonade and strife were done,
  The power of Kings was felt no more,
Above them shone the summer sun -
  A Nation's birth hovered before.

The farmer left behind his plow,
  The lawyer from his clients fled,
And over every patriot brow
  The halo of high purpose spread.

The merchant then forgot his trade,
  To desk and house the summons flew,
Here, largely, was that compact made,
  Firmer than any Empire knew.

Great are the victories of war,
  But greater - when its battles cease -
Are those high ends men battle for -
  The halcyon victories of peace.

Such men as Agamemnon saw,
   Were they - or those in Plato's realm -
Who strove to perfect Freedom's law,
   Who stood as heroes at the helm.

What if, among their various minds,
   Sharp difference led to sharp debate;
No worthy cause a triumph finds
   Unless the toil and thought be great.

Even Greece and Rome, enshrined in fame,
   Who taught the world how men were ruled,
Had none who put our own to shame -
   None more endowed, or better schooled.

We may not see what gave them fear,
   What spectres made their counsels wait;
We only know that we are here,
   And owe to them our happy fate.

Ours are the vision and the proof,
   Theirs was a problem full of doubt,
And those who feared and held aloof,
   Did much to work it wisely out.

The dissidents who lingered long
   Before they caught the Union ring,
Felt, maybe, that a league too strong
   Might build the ladder for a King.

They saw the summer wear away
   Before their noble work was done;
No matter, - we who meet to-day
   Reap now the fruits their wisdom won.

A hundred years! How short this seems
   When one who sits upon this stage
Shook hands with one whose patriot dreams
   Were fashioned in that very age.

I almost see the couriers come

With cheering news from other states,
Which shaped, beneath the Court-house dome,
  The happy end of those debates -

And stirred the hearts of men who strove
  To make this Union just and strong:
'Twas wrought through links of law and love -
  Heaven grant that it may prosper long.

I see the little hamlet here -
  Your city now upon a hill -
The same sweet, summer atmosphere
  That crowned its glory, crowns it still.

Its men were true as ever live;
  Its women fair as mortal meets, -
Quite like our modern girls who give
  Famed beauty to Poughkeepsie's streets.

But who can treat a topic, fraught
  With hints that bankrupt speech and rhyme?
That feature needs no poet's thought
  Which lives transparent through all time!

A hundred years! They pass to night
  Where the soft sunset paints the west, -
And now another century's flight
  Dawns, with its wonders all unguessed.

The fathers sleep. 'Tis ours to do -
  And cherish well their sacred trust,
And pass it on to centuries new
  When we, as they, are given to dust.

O bind it to the future, far
  As time's long scroll runs on before, -
Fast as your bridge with bolt and bar
  Shall span the Hudson, shore to shore.

Hallowe'en

Joel Benton

Pixie, kobold, elf, and sprite,
All are on their rounds to-night;
In the wan moon's silver ray,
Thrives their helter-skelter play.

Fond of cellar, barn, or stack,
True unto the almanac,
They present to credulous eyes
Strange hobgoblin mysteries.

Cabbage-stumps - straws wet with dew -
Apple-skins, and chestnuts too,
And a mirror for some lass
Show what wonders come to pass.

Doors they move, and gates they hide;
Mischiefs that on moonbeams ride
Are their deeds - and, by their spells,
Love records its oracles.

Don't we all, of long ago,
By the ruddy fireplace glow,
In the kitchen and the hall,
Those queer, cooflike pranks recall?

Eery shadows were they then -
But to-night they come again;
Were we once more but sixteen
Precious would be Hallowe'en.

The Winter Woods

Joel Benton

In the dense forest where the squirrel lives,
   And somber shadows fill the tree roofed space;
Where nature her still benediction gives,
   And the dead year lays off its crown of grace -
How restful, to one tired with city streets,
   To watch the frolic of the chickadee,
To feel the leaf packed carpet, and to chase
   The silver runnel, gurgling to the sea.

There are no splendors that were seen in May,
   I find no laurel tinct by opulent June;
But in the bleak, dun February day,
   With the caw of crows and the sharp air in tune,
I love to wait till the northern trumpets blow,
   And homeward walk through flakes of riotous snow.

Grandmother's Garden

Joel Benton

Did you know it (what visions its memory unlocks!),
With its beds of bright pansies and quaint four-o-clocks?
For the newfangled blossoms we dote on to-day
Have driven our grandmother's garden away.

There were wonders within it, scarce known now, galore.
Its bright morning-glories crept up to the door;
Prim balsams, sweet pinks, feverfew, marigold,
And many-hued poppies, a sight to behold.

Its beds and its walks geometric were laid;
The box on its borders seemed out for parade;
Gay tulips in masses, or bunched as deemed best,
Were gorgeous and stately, and royally dressed.

Geraniums, larkspur, and peonies bold, -
The last daring sometimes the snow and the cold, -
Canterbury-bells white, and likewise the blue,
Were favorite flowers that our grandmothers knew.

Sweet-brier, honeysuckle, and tuberoses rare
Were lovingly nurtured, and tended with care;
Clove-pink, lady-slipper, spiced fennel and dill,
And caraway, too. I remember them still.

Buttercups, clematis, nasturtium, sweet pea,
(The last has survived for the youngsters to see),
And balm, for winged callers that sought it in flocks;
Sweet-william and lychnis, and pink and white phlox.

Velvet dahlias and asters and cockscomb beside,
And mases of hollyhocks flaming in pride;
Even snowballs and sunflowers, if not of rare grace,
Rose boldly to show that they, too, had a place.

Syringas and hyacinths these caught the dew

And the sun - and the "marvel (so called) of Peru'"
What an army! Too many to singly recall.
But our grandmother's garden could welcome them all.

The lilac of springtime is ever in mind;
Its fame is as broad as the range of mankind;
Long linked with the thoughts of our earliest years,
Its faint luscious odor brings rapture and tears.

You may boast of the Latin-named flowers of to-day,
And the leaf-beds that make such a dashing display;
But I mourn for time's havoc, and long to restore
The garden that bloomed by our grandmother's door.

Horatio Nelson Powers
(1826-1890)

Horatio Nelson Powers was born in
Amenia and as a youth, attended Amenia
Seminary. After graduating from Union
College in Schenectady, he began a long
career as an Episcopal rector serving in
Pennsylvania, Illinois, Iowa, Connecticut, and New York.

Outside his career in the church, Powers maintained a thriving literary
life as a poet and essayist whose work appeared in numerous periodi-
cals. He also wrote a biography of his friend William Cullen Bryant
and served as president of Griswold College in Iowa and regent of the
University of Chicago.

As a noteworthy minor poet of his era, Powers' work was often antholo-
gized in popular poetry collections of his day. In the following three po-
ems, Powers reflects upon his youth in Dutchess County and two of the
county's natural wonders (Dover Stone Church and the Hudson River)
whose effect upon him was profound.

Youth

Horatio Nelson Powers

O radiant land! where my young eyes
Saw angels in the happy skies,
And felt Love's arms in all the air,
And heard Hope singing everywhere -
Sweet land of boyhood! Rose unblown!
Delicious, heart-enfolded Zone!
    How soon - too soon
    The burning Noon
Drank all thy dew from bud and leaf
And seared the bowers of young Belief.

- A Birthday Lyric

The Hudson

Horatio Nelson Powers

O the eyes that glowed bright in the spell of thy beauty,
    When summers were sweetest in Hope's luscious clime!
O the hearts that, on errands of honor and duty,
    Were braced by thy grandeurs, O, river sublime!

O the loves and the dreams that were born where thy glories
    In sunset and moonlight their witchery wore,
While the warm lips of youth breathed the tenderest stories
    Into ears that still listened in rapture for more!

O the worn, and the weary, who, coming and going
    Have watched thy repose through the mist of their tears!
O the gallant and wise who, with garlands still growing,
    Will hallow thy banks till the earth disappears!

I think of the anguish, now ended and over,
    Of lonely ones journeying here with their dead;
Of patriot, scholar, and traitor, and lover,
    And poems in hearts that have never been read.

I think, as I picture the mighty procession
    Of beauty, and genius, of greatness and fame,
That here passed, up and down, with a ceaseless progression,
    How empty the honors of station and name!

I summon the faces, the numberless faces
    That were turned to thee fondly, as onward they sped
To their labors, their pleasures, their fireside places,
    And am dazed by the manifold meanings they shed.

How the air seems to vibrate with sorrow and laughter,
    The hopes and the gladness, the griefs and despair
Of those who have failed, and those who flee after
    The phantom of Joy that they dream is so fair.

O beauty that glowed in the rose of our morning!

O the promise that shone when our pathway was new!
O blossom of love, our high noontide adorning,
   What a splendor o'er all this fair region ye threw!

I thrill with the vision, with the stress of emotion,
   As the swarm of the pageants, O Hudson, appear;
And yet, as a child dips his cup in the ocean,
   I receive but a sip of the glory that's here.

The Stone Church

Horatio Nelson Powers

Our path has been beside a mountain stream,
Up through a weird and wonderous ravine,
'Neath fragrant canopies of ancient trees,
And 'tween green tasseled rocks, that, 'mong the ferns,
Sleep like old Titans.

      On the left arise
Huge, massy ramparts of eternal cliff,
Ragged and steep, with many a green recess
And fissure dark: Across the creek, upon
The swift slope of the mountain's jagged side,
Spread out the solemn groves wide-branched and dim
As old Cathedrals. But right on in front
The frowning perpendicular of rock
Expands, mid clustering festoons of thick leaves,
Into a noble vestibule, whose walls
Rise in an arched and adamantine dome.
Like a large, lustrous eye of blue, the sky
Looks in a blessing through the parted roof.

  On 'neath the Gothic portal do we pass,
Up the dim aisle, above the dashing fall,
Whose white spray softens the melodious air,
'Till, passing thro' a narrow granite hall
We tread a spacious theatre of stone.
This is the Church. Its daedal walls are hung
As for a festival with laurel boughs,
With pendulous tresses of long moss and fern,
Bright tufts of grass, and sweet half buried flowers,
High crowned with gnarled and overleaning trees.
Dark, fallen cliffs are in the centre piled,
Most pulpit-like and stern. Swift from above
A silver cascade slides down to the floor,
With liquid syllables of lulling sound -

Chanting the hymn that Nature at its birth
Poured through its soft and music-loving lips.
Far over all, the sweet and tremulous sky
Bends its embracing canopy of love.

Here Nature seems at prayer; and as you gaze
On her lone altar mid the list'ning hills,
And hear the ceaseless symphonies that float
From woods and waters on the cool sweet air,
You feel that holier aspirations steal
Into the willing heart - your subtler thought,
Tranced in the Benediction brooding round,
Glows half inspired with its unuttered praise.

(1851)

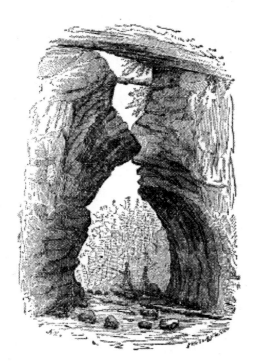

Illustration: Dover Stone Church 1877

Dr. Edward Hazen Parker
(1823-1896)

Dr. Edward Hazen Parker spent almost 40 years of his life as a highly respected Poughkeepsie surgeon and family physician. Twice a professor, father of five, one time President of the New York State Medical Society, hospital trustee, church vestryman, and sometime poet, Dr. Parker's life seemed praiseworthy but not particularly unusual - that is, until 1881. In that year, to Dr. Parker's surprise, four lines from one of his poems were inscribed prominently on a tablet at the head of assassinated United States President James A. Garfield's coffin. These four simples lines, reprinted around the globe, read:

> Life's race well run,
> Life's work well done,
> Life's crown well won,
>   Now comes rest.

Dr. Parker noted that the lines were slightly incorrect, but assumed someone had simply misremembered his poem published the year before in the *New York Observer*.

The sudden and completely unexpected international prominence of his poem had remarkably little effect on the busy doctor. He recollected later that, "I was gratified that they [the four lines of poetry] should have thus lingered in anyone's memory; I thought no more about it."[1]

Other people, however, thought plenty about it. Several people came forward claiming authorship, and the situation grew so confused that journalists in President Garfield's hometown of Cleveland, Ohio set out to find the author of the poem that had touched so many.

With wry good humor, Dr. Parker from Poughkeepsie eventually came forward to tell his own story - joking that he was in fact "that Parker, whoever he is." He humbly wrote,

> May I add a few words concerning the lines and their history? They were written early in 1879, on the occasion of the death of a valued

friend of myself and my family, being the result of reflections on her busy, useful, Christian life, when I found myself obliged to take daily a long drive to see a patient. Medical men, I apprehend, do a large share of their thinking at such times; at any rate, I know I do. They were printed for convenience, that they might be sung at the funeral of my wife's mother, which occurred a few months later, and it was then, I suppose, that my friend, Professor Crosby, first saw them. It was at his request that they were printed in the *New York Observer* about a year af-terward. At that time our names were attached to them - his to the Latin, and mine to the English version.[2]

Although bemused by the whole experience, Dr. Parker could not help but register mild dismay that these four famous lines had been cut adrift from the rest of his poem and that they were in fact slightly different from his original version. Nonetheless, he acknowledged that "...it touches me deeply that these simple lines have reached so many hearts." [3]

Once commonly known as "Garfield's epitaph," the first four lines of Dr. Parker's poem have been translated into many languages and continue to turn up in eulogies and on gravestones.

"There remaineth therefore a rest to the people of God."

Dr. Edward Hazen Parker

Life's race well run,
Life's work all done,
Life's victory won,
  Now cometh rest.

Sorrows are o'er,
Trials no more,
Ship reacheth shore,
  Now cometh rest.

Faith yields to sight,
Day follows night,
Jesus gives light,
  Now cometh rest.

We awhile wait,
But, soon or late,
Death opes the gate,
  Then cometh rest.

(Although it later became known world wide, this poem was originally written to celebrate the life of a now long forgotten Poughkeepsian named Lydia Ingraham Phinney whose remarkable ministering to the needs of Poughkeepsie's Christ Church inspired Dr. Parker's poem. A bronze cross carved with passion flowers still hangs in the church's south transept in memory of Miss Phinney.)

The challenge of capturing in words both the beauty and danger of ice yachting has long attracted writers, including Dr. Parker in the poem that follows written in March, 1883. Local historian and Vassar College president, Henry Noble MacCracken noted the strong connection between ice yachting and poetry in this description from his 1958 book Blithe Dutchess:

There seems no doubt that Poughkeepsie was [ice yachting's] first home in America. Dutchess never came nearer to poetry, than when her artisans designed the ice yacht...When George Buckhout of Poughkeepsie sailed a measured mile and a half in 32 seconds, at 176 miles per hour, he was entering a new dimension for the human imagination... Their poetry came out in the yacht's names...These were Flying Cloud, Northern Light, Haze, North Star, Meteor, Snowflake, and Hail. There were the Zero, Blue Streak, Icicle, Blitzen, Scud, Puff, and Whiff. There were the Dart, Flyaway, Dash, and Zigzag... [4]

The Race of the Ice Yachts

Dr. Edward Hazen Parker

I

Ho! for the yachts, Hoho!
The ice is smooth,
The breeze is fair
The day is bright
Crisp is the air:
Ho for the yachts! Hoho!

II

Hurrah for the race! Hurrah!
Eager they come to win the prize,
Flitting about like butterflies;
Gliding along to try their speed -
Going about (take heed, take heed),
So quickly that each must need
A cool head in the willer,
A strong hand on the tiller:
For perils and dangers
Surround these swift rangers -
Hurrah for the race! Hurrah!

III

See how the yachts now slowly range in line,
And note what beauties in their forms combine,
The slender spars, the snow white sails,
  The polished metals of their rails,
   The brilliant pennon borne by each,
   As 'twere a sprite, that strives to reach
   A speed so much beyond its own,
   Or that which bird has ever known:
   But only dares aloft to perch,
   Fearful of peril in its search.

IV

With bowsprits to the wind,
Ready the helm to mind,
Panting their course to find,
   They stand in row,
   Ready to go,
   O'er ice or snow;
Whenever the word is given.

V

AEolus and Maze,
Jack Frost and Haze,
Hesperus, Icicle, Whirlwind, Kildare,
   Gracie and Scud,
   Snowdrift and Maud,
Avalanche, Cyclone and Snowbird are there.

VI

"Sail four times over the course - five miles
"From East to west turn goals meanwhiles;
"Put one man on the runner plank;
"Don't go too near the western bank.
"Or you will surely lose the wind,
"And find yourself left far behind."
       So the instructions ran.

VII

The signal given round they go,
And, swift as arrows from the bow,
Shot o'er the sparkling ice;
  Forward and back
  With frequent tack
Threading a tangled maze;
  Now luffing, now filling,
  Now jibing, as willing
  All beholders to daze;
And the goals have been rounded twice.

VIII

Again they traverse the lengthy course,
Faster than any racing horse,
  Hear how they hum
  As down they come;
  Sheets hauled tight
  That each gust may bite;

Windward runner in the air, -
Ah, tis a sight so rare
That one may wisely fear to tell,
Unless his listeners know him well,
  How his veins filled
  How his nerves thrilled;
As he watched the ice yacht race.

IX

Now down they come the final time,
Throwing up sprays of whitest rime.
  Make out if you can
  Who heads the van,
    Aeolus? No!
    Gracie? Not so!
    Where is Kildare?
    No where! No where!
    Jack Frost and Haze
    Are leading the maze,
    Which one will beat?
    It seems a dead heat:
    But soon 'twill be told
    If this pace they hold:
Hurrah! Jack Frost crosses the line.

X

Then as the men come thronging about
Together they raise a ringing shout
  "Jack Frost is king;" -
And the snow clad hills around
Echo back with solemn sound
  "Jack Frost is king;" -
While from the depths of the great river,
Making its icy fetters quiver,
  Comes a low moan,
  A sullen groan,
  "Jack Frost is king."

Wallace Bruce *(1844-1914)*

Wallace Bruce was born in Hillsdale, in New York's Columbia County and graduated from Yale in 1867. After a brief stint studying law and travelling in Europe, Bruce settled in Poughkeepsie at age 27 to "adopt Literature and Lecturing as his life work" (as his press agents later put it). As an orator for hire working in every region of the country, he soon began a traveller's life. But for over twenty years, Bruce returned after each lecture tour to his home on Franklin Street in Poughkeepsie.

As one of the era's leading orators, Bruce blended humor, poetry and inspirational patriotism in lectures full of what one critic called the "throbbing life of the 19th century." His lectures were sometimes literary (Burns, Scott and Shakespeare), but also motivational with titles like "Native Mettle," "Ready Wit" and "Genius and Work."

At the height of his career, Bruce's lecture circuit covered 26 states with performances at Chautauqua gatherings, centennials, lyceum meetings, torchlight parades, dedications, reunions, and institutional anniversaries. Speaking without notes, Bruce's voice was described as soulful and full of fire - clear and audible even outdoors among crowds sometimes numbering in the thousands.

The *Brooklyn Times* described one of Bruce's show stopping appearances:

> When he spoke of 'making two words of noblemen,' wild and long was the patriotic shouting. Mr. Bruce recited with the fervor of a minstrel chanting the deeds of gods and heroes, and on retiring to his seat the merits of his composition and his inspiring earnestness were recognized with cheers, and a score of men, whose eyes had moistened and their faces flushed while they listened to him, sprang forward to shake him by the hand.[1]

In 1889, Bruce was appointed U.S. Consul to Edinburgh, Scotland where he brought about the creation of a memorial to Scottish soldiers who fought for the Union Army in the American Civil War. The memorial statue (of Lincoln and a freed slave) was designed by Poughkeepsie sculptor George Bissell and stands in the Calton Cemetery in Edinburgh.

Bruce's love of the Hudson River was what first drew him to Poughkeepsie even though he later recollected that he had known "not a single person, nor did a single person know me" when he first arrived.

His interest in the Hudson brought him great success as a writer of Hudson River guidebooks in which he was the first to describe Poughkeepsie as "Queen City of the Hudson" - a phrase still remembered today.[2] Few people, however, recall that it was the 19th century poet and orator Wallace Bruce who coined this phrase.

To My Wife

Wallace Bruce

I have in life but wishes three:
The first is realized in thee;

The second you can surely guess -
Sweet presents sent from Heaven to bless;

The third some sweet and quiet nook,
To read the leaves of Nature's book.

I could not make my wishes four -
Love, children, home - Earth has no more.

Poughkeepsie

Wallace Bruce

There was a young man in Pokipsie
Who liked a certain girl's lipsie;
    But her papa came in,
    And the young man did a spin
Right down the front steps as if tipsy.

There was a young lady at Vassar
As learned as any professor;
    She wore her dress plain,
    To show she had brain,
And she would not let any one "sass" her.

There was at the big Eastman College
A youth so crammed full of knowledge,
    When he opened his jaw
    He filled you with awe,
And you left without any apolege.

(This poem appeared in Bruce's From the Hudson to the Yosemite *published in 1884 and was accompanied by the following sly introduction with its reference to the Poughkeepsie train station: "It has been regarded for more than a century that the word Poughkeepsie, derived from the Indian 'Apo-keep-sing,' signified 'Safe Harbor;' but, after patient investigation, it is now generally understood that the original meaning was simply 'Ten Minutes for Refreshments'...")*

Tulips

Wallace Bruce

Where grows the flower, and what's its name,
That blooms in winter and summer the same?
The language of which some say is true,
Some say is false; now what say you?

Pray sing not of florals that wither and fade
When crimson and gold on the woodlands are laid,
And Autumn unfurls on the deep mountain-side
His banners rich-woven and brilliantly dyed.
One flower, and one only, earth's frost never nips
On hill-side or valley - the sweet two-lips.

In fairest of gardens, in nooks growing wild,
In cold Arctic climes where the rose never smiled,
Where bright waters flow, where soft breezes blow,
In lands that are wrapped in perpetual snow,
They bloom in rich beauty, for sunlight or shade
Despoils not their sweetness, nor makes them to fade;
And, furthermore, reader, this also is true -
Whenever they're pressed they blossom anew.

A Wanderer

Wallace Bruce

I have wandered the wide world o'er,
   I have sailed over many a sea,
But the land that I love more and more
   Is Columbia, the land of the free;
From the east to the western shore,
   From the north to the southern sea,
      Columbia for me!

I have lingered in ivy-grown bowers,
   In minsters and palaces vast,
Amid castles and crumbling towers
   Whose shadows backward are cast;
But the longed-for Atlantis is ours,
   And freedom interprets at last
      The dream of the past.

The rivers of story and song,
   The Danube, the Elbe, and the Rhine,
Entrance for a day, but I long
   For the dear old Hudson of mine;
The Hudson, where memories throng,
   Where love's fondest tendrils entwine,
      Of beauty the shrine.

Like music entranced in a dream
   Glide the Afton, the Doon and the Ayr;
But the Jansen, the clear Jansen stream,
   In one heart shall their melody share;
And my soul still reflects its bright gleam,
   For I played in my childhood there,
      When visions were fair.

I heard the sweet chiming of bells,
   From the Seine to the Avon and Dee;
But sweeter the anthem that swells,
   From the pine-clad Sierras to me;

And the Sabbath-like stillness that dwells
   In these mountains far up from the sea;
      Lake Tahoe with thee.

I have gathered sweet flowers in the west,
   Where the streams are embroidered with gold;
But the blossoms that I love the best
   Are those which I gathered of old;
The same that my mother's lips pressed,
   Their petals the sweetness still hold,
      Her heart they enfold.

I have wandered the wide world o'er,
   I have sailed over many a sea,
But the land that I love more and more
   Is Columbia, the land of the free;
From the east to the western shore,
   From the north to the southern sea,
      Columbia for me!

The following poem was read by Bruce in 1884 at the 25th Anniversary of Poughkeepsie's Eastman Business College. A local newspaper described the scene that day:

A magnificent audience packed the Opera House Friday evening, the occasion being the annual anniversary address before the students of Eastman National Business College. The stage was very handsomely decorated with tropical plants, and festooned and hung with flags, while to the right was a large portrait of the late H.G. Eastman. The 400 students marched to the Opera House in line, took seats in the orchestra chairs and in the first circle of the parquet, those seats having been reserved for them. Ladies and gentlemen were arriving every moment and before the hour fixed for the exercises to begin, had filled the entire parquet, family circle and part of the upper gallery. The elite of the city were there, and the scene was a brilliant one...Wallace Bruce was introduced and recited elegantly the following poem written by him for the occasion...When Mr. Bruce finished the applause was loud and long. (Poughkeepsie Daily Eagle: September 20, 1884)

"Shall Stand With Kings"*

Wallace Bruce

From out the turmoil and the strife
   Of party clamor fierce and wide,
From quiet homes and restful life,
   We gather here with honest pride,

To note the hour, to mark the year,
   Our "Business College" had its birth,
To emphasize with hearty cheer
   Our recognition of its worth;

To place the never-dying flowers
   Of love upon its founder's brow,
To make his zeal and courage ours,
   Twin-words which still these walls endow;

*Proverbs 22:29: "He who is diligent in business shall stand with kings; he shall not stand with mean men."

To stand beside the corner-stone,
　　The base our Eastman laid so well,
To note the work so ably done
　　By you on whom his mantle fell;

To bring with warm and grateful hearts
　　An offering from Poughkeepsie due -
Queen City of a hundred marts,
　　Midway between the mountains blue;

Between the On-ti-o-ras grand, -
　　The Catskills grouped like Titans old,
And Highlands firm, whose Beacons stand
　　To watch the morning tints unfold;

Midway the Hudson's glorious tide
　　"Safe Harbor" - Apo-keep-sing reads -
An anchorage sure, with outlook wide,
　　Midway between your dreams and deeds.

From vigorous youth to manhood bold
　　Your college passes now to-night,
Its twenty-five years proudly told
　　In living letters clear and bright.

It turns the quarter-flag and post
　　With bounding strength and quickening pace,
While sturdy shout and valid boast
　　Proclaim it foremost in the race.

And you who form the present link
　　Within this ever-lengthening chain,
From far Sierra's mountain brink
　　From coral reefs to pine-clad Maine,

From northern coast, from sunny lands,
　　From Aztec cities old and gray,
From Nicaragua's burning sands -
　　You take no idle part to-day.

You, too, are near your manhoods' line

The quarter-post is also yours,
Whereon these words transparent shine -
   Unceasing toil success insures.

There's room enough on every hand
   For men of muscle, brain, and nerve;
Supply ne'er met the loud demands
   Of honesty too high to swerve.

The field you enter on is wide,
   You make the laws that statesmen frame,
You hold secure the reins that guide
   The nations' course to power and fame.

You lift the torch and bridge the stream
   Whereon with wonder centuries look;
You frame and sell the artist's dream,
   You bind and ship the poet's book.

Through granite rocks you drive apace,
Round mountain-peaks your girdles wind,
Your desk and table span the space
   Between material and mind.

You bring the coinage of the world
   To Lombard Street from India's sun,
And France her proud tricolor furled
   To London's gold, not Wellington.

"The man in business diligent
   Shall stand with kings:" remaineth true;
To Jewish wealth Napoleon bent -
   Rothschild was king at Waterloo.

His word was "open sesame"
   To banker's vault and miser's hoard;
His signature proved literally,
   "The pen is mightier than the sword."

But in the race for power and fame,
   The eager striving for success,

Mark this - true love and honest name
　　Confer the only happiness.

The house that's founded on a wrong
　　Is built and reared at fearful cost,
And judgment falls, though waiting long,
　　On honors gained by honor lost.

Festina lente! haste but wait!
　　Have patience though the hour-sands waste;
It seems the paradox of fate
　　To hold in check and bid us haste.

Be bold, ay, bold, but not too bold,
　　Is sung again in verses new;
Despise not truths and maxims old,
　　Be upright, faithful, firm, and true.

Let conscience, trust, and rectitude
　　Forever in your hearts abide,
And may Life's Book of debts accrued
　　Find balance on the credit side!

Photo:Eastman Business College
(New York Public Library)

Clover and Heather

Wallace Bruce

There are greetings the wide world over,
  And blossoms wherever we roam,
But none like the heather and clover
  To welcome the wanderer home.

Warm-hearted with kindred devotion,
  Twin sisters in sympathy true,
They whisper across the wide ocean,
  Love-laden with memory's dew.

In purple tints woven together
  The Hudson shakes hand with the Tweed,
Commingling with Abbotsford's heather
  The clover of Sunnyside's mead.

A token of friendship immortal
  With Washington Irving returns -
Scott's ivy entwined o'er his portal
  By the "Blue-eyed Lassie" of Burns.

Their names by heather-bells wedded
  With fondness Columbia retains;
In freedom's foundation imbedded
  The lay of the minstrel remains.

Ay, this their commission and glory,
  In redolent bloom to prolong
Love, liberty, legend, and story,
  That blossom in ballad and song.

So here's to the clover and heather
  Of riverside, mountain and glen,
As I stand wi' doffed bonnet and feather
  At the yett of my forbears again.

Memorial-Day

Wallace Bruce

I come with chaplet woven new
From May-day flowers, to fade away;
You come to-night, brave boys in blue,
With record bright, to last for aye.

Yet all I have I gladly bring
With heart and voice at your command;
I only wish the words I sing
Were worthier of your noble band –

A living wreath of lasting fame
To match your deeds that fill the world.
Ah, lyric vain! Each hero's name
Is on your banners' fold unfurled.

Those stars are there in setting blue,
Because you answered to the call.
We bring no eulogy to you;
You honor us – you won it all.

And what avails our words of praise
To you who stand as in a dream
On guard in rugged mountain ways,
In camp by many a sluggish stream!

Among the clouds on Lookout Height,
With Hooker down in Tennesee;
Again the boys "mit Sigel fight,"
You march with Sherman to the sea.

Port Hudson, Vicksburg, New Orleans,
Antietam, Shiloh, Malvern Hill –
A hundred fields, a thousand scenes
The moistened lens of memory fill.

On fields with Grant, whose grave is white
With flowers from many a distant State,

Through many a long and weary night
You learned with him to toil and wait.

And there with Hancock, soldier true,
At Gettysburg you held the line;
No nobler heart beneath the blue,
For him the nations' flowers entwine.

Brave captain, noble comrades, rest!
No bugle note or war's alarms
Disturb your sleep on Nature's breast –
That silent camp of grounded arms.

Your ranks are thin, boys, to-day
Than just one little year ago;
On many a brow a touch of gray
Anticipates the winter's snow.

And fewer comrades year by year,
Shall gather summer's kindly bloom
And fewer brothers drop the tear
Upon the soldier's sacred tomb.

The twenty years have left their trace
Since you returned the homeward route;
Twice twenty more your ranks efface;
The boys will all be mustered out,

Who kept the faith and fought the fight;
The glory theirs, the duty ours;
They earned the crown, the hero's right
The victor's wreath – a crown of flowers.

(Read at Poughkeepsie, 1886)

William Harloe (1818-1891)

William Harloe was born in Dublin but grew up in New York where he apprenticed with his immigrant father in the building trades. He began his own career on Staten Island, where he is said to have built the Jacob Vanderbilt estate "Clove Hill."

Harloe settled in Poughkeepsie in the late 1850s and for the next 30 years, was known as an "outspoken and determined" citizen as well as an ambitious and highly capable builder and self-taught architect. [1]

Many of Poughkeepsie's finest mid-Victorian churches were built by William Harloe including the superb Holy Comforter Church (designed in 1859 by the great Cathedral architect Richard Upjohn), St. Paul's Episcopal Church (designed in 1872 by New York architect Emlin T. Littel), Washington Street M.E. Church (built in 1859, demolished in 1968), and the German Lutheran Church (built in 1866, now vacant).

Harloe is perhaps best known as the builder of the Vassar's Main Building and Observatory, two of the college's original buildings completed by 1864. Also surviving are Harloe's Poughkeepsie brownstones - restored in 2002 and still known as "Harloe Row." The home he built for himself and his own family is also still standing at 16 Davies Place opposite his beloved Holy Comforter Church where he was an active congregant and church leader.

Although deeply invested in Poughkeepsie (Harloe was even elected Mayor in 1879), he appears to have been an active builder in Manhattan as well, although his career there has yet to be fully documented. As a poet, Harloe wrote under the pen name "Veritas," and his work was frequently published in local papers of the period.

The Church Building

William Harloe

Count well the cost - select the site;
  Strip off each flower and sod,
In humble prayer, bid all unite
  To bless the house designed for God,
Dig foundation broad and deep,
  Cautiously preserve the level,
Close, edge to edge, the base-stones keep,
  And concrete well each interval.

Dress every Ashlar, square and true,
  Starting from its bottom bed;
From every stone the roughness hew,
  Ready now, cement to spread;
In bonded union, every stone
  Sustains and keeps the other,
The building now is well begun,
  Cemented all together.

Now Step by Step, the massive pile
The tired craftsmen rest a-while
  Slowly rises higher,
  To Worship and admire;
Refreshment o'er, each in his place
  With skill performs his part,
Fresh efforts crown with Beauty's grace
  The Noble work of Art.

In Strength and Beauty still it grows
  With steady measured march,
Right level gain'd, the "Trestle" shows
  It ready for the Arch;
Each Keystone set, each Arch completes
  A United strong entirety.
All rest, well pleased each other greets,
  Then onward to maturity.

St. Paul's Episcopal (1872)

Washington M.E. Church (1859)

German Lutheran Church (1866)

The boldest workmen now repair
  To build the lofty spire;
Onward, upward, still they dare,
  Higher yet, still higher;
Selected craftsmen every one,
  True Master of his part,
Raise up, and set the topmost stone
  That crowns the work of Art.

The glowing Cross is planted high;
  The Christian's emblem, and the sign,
That lifts the mortal to the sky,
  To praise the Architect divine;
The weary Pilgrims oft will stop
  To greet the sign of Victory,
The Red Cross on the Temple's top,
  The Badge of Christian heraldry.

The Temple's built, The Cross on high,
Victorious Sign, salutes the sky,
Throw wide the doors, admit the throng,
The Temple fill with joyous song,
Lift Heavenly Anthems high, and swell
The praises of Emmanuel.

Holy Comforter Church (1859)

Josh Billings (1818-1885)

When the great 19th century humorist Josh Billings arrived in Poughkeepsie in 1858, he was already 40 years old. Since age 15, he had lived what he referred to as a "border life" - opting out of the well connected and comfortable world of his parents to pursue a wandering life of adventure. He had explored the west, piloted a steamboat, farmed the land, and mined for coal - but never once had he considered writing for publication.

In 1858, the stage persona and pen name "Josh Billings" was yet to be born, and Poughkeepsie townsfolk knew Billings only by his real name, Henry Wheeler Shaw. But with his striking looks and sly quick wit, Shaw soon stood out - especially in his highly visible role as local auctioneer. The editor of the local paper even encouraged Shaw to write a newspaper column, assuring him that "anybody who can talk like you can, can also write." [1]

One of Shaw's very first columns, titled "Essay on a Mule," was later to become one of his most quoted pieces and a personal favorite of Abraham Lincoln. At first, however, only Poughkeepsie papers printed his work. Frustrated, Shaw decided to adopt the pen name of "Josh Billings" and resubmit his columns using the bad spelling and poor grammar of a backwoods illiterate. Using his "Josh Billings" persona, Shaw explained: "I hold that a man has just as much rite tew spel a word as it is pronounced, as he has tew pronounce it the way it ain't spelt."

With this clever "backwoods" presentation of his particular brand of humor, Shaw's work soon caught the attention of publishers. But Shaw's local fans in Poughkeepsie saw that there might be even more in store for their local auctioneer-turned-writer and coaxed him to condense his essays into a lyceum lecture. In the minister's study in the back of Poughkeepsie's Congregational Church, one of America's soon to be great comic lecturers made his first attempt at performing.[2]

At over six feet in height with a slouching walk and trademark felt hat - his long flowing hair tucked behind his ears and an absurdly gloomy expression on his face - Henry W. Shaw transformed himself into the rustic American philosopher "Josh Billings." His lectures, with titles like "Milk," "What I Know about Hotels" and "The Pensive Cockroach," contained epigrams, proverbs and anecdotes that were gleefully told and retold all across America. His most quoted "affurism" remains, "It is better to kno less, than to kno so mutch that ain't so."

Throughout the 1870s, Billings was delivering roughly 80 lectures per year and writing for newspapers, magazines and book publishers with enormous success. As time passed, however, readers were put off by the slow process of deciphering Billing's phonetic spellings. Today his work is no longer well known, though during his lifetime, he rivaled the likes of Mark Twain and Artemus Ward in public popularity.

Once he had become a successful author and lecturer, Billings left Poughkeepsie but frequently returned to visit his elderly mother and the local friends who were first to recognize his tremendous talent. His knowledge of the Hudson Valley (at least partly attained through his work as land agent) is apparent in this spoof of a local real estate ad:

> I kan sell for eighteen hundred and thirty-nine dollars, a pallas, a sweet and pensive retirement, lokated on the virgin banks ov the Hudson, kontaining 85 acres. The land is luxuriously divided by the hand of natur and art, into pastor and tillage, into plain and deklivity, into stern abruptness, and the dallianse ov moss-tufted medders - streams ov sparkling gladness (thick with trout) danse through this wilderness ov buty, tew the low musik of the kricket and grasshopper. The evergreen sighs as the evening zephir flits through its shadowy buzzum, and the aspen trembles like the luv-smitten harte ov a damsell...The manshun iz ov Parian marble, the porch iz a single diamond, set with rubiz and mother ov pearl; the floors are ov rosewood, and the ceilings are more butiful than the starry vault of heavin. Hot and cold water bubbles and squirts in evry apartment and nothing is wanted that a poet could pra for, or art could portray. The stables are worthy ov the steeds ov Nimrod, or the stud ov Akilles, and its henery was bilt expressly for the birds of paradice; while somber in the distance, like the cave ov a hermit, glimpses are caught of the dorg-house. Here poets hav cum and warbled their laze - here skulptors hav cut, here painters have robbed the scene of dreamy landskapes...Walls ov primitiff rock, laid in Roman cement, bound the estate while upward and downward, the eye catches far away the magesta and slow grander ov the Hudson. As the young moon hangs like a cutting ov silver from the blu brest ov the ski, an angel may be seen each night dansing with golden tiptoes on

the green. (N.B. This angel goes with the place.) [3]

Several months before his death, Billings looked back on his literary career and attributed his success not to any great originality, but rather to his comical backwoods delivery of practical American wisdom. His attempts at poetry, he described with self-deprecating humor:

> Manifess destiny iz a diseasze, but it is eazy tew heal; I hav seen it in its wust stages cured bi sawing a cord ov dri hickory wood. I thought i had it onse, it broke out in the shape ov poetry; i sent a speciment ov the desseaze tew a magazine, the magazine man wrote me next day as follers: 'Dear Sur: Yu may be a darn phule, but yu are no poeck. Yures, in haste.' [4]

Upon Billings death in 1885, James Whitcomb Riley wrote the following poem as a grateful memorial to a man whose humor was once considered an American treasure.

Illustration: from Josh Billing's Old Farmer's Allminax (*1871*)
"The Man whom you kant
git to write poetry or
tell the truth until you
git him haff drunk aint
worth the investment -
no sir, Josh Billings"

Josh Billings

James Whitcomb Riley

DEAD IN CALIFORNIA, OCTOBER 15, 1885

Jolly-hearted old Josh Billings,
  With his wisdom and his wit,
And his gravity of presence,
  And the drollery of it!
Has he left us, and forever?
  When so many merry years
He has only left us laughing -
And he leaves us now in tears?

Has he turned from his "Deer Publik,"
  With his slyly twinkling eyes
Now grown dim and heavy-lidded
  In despite of sunny skies? -
Yet with rugged brow uplifted,
  And the long hair tossed away,
Like an old heroic lion,
  With a mane of iron-gray.

Though we lose him, still we find him
  In the mirth of every lip,
And we fare through all his pages
  In his glad companionship:
His voice is wed with Nature's
  Laughing in each woody nook
With the chirrup of the robin
  And the chuckle of the brook.

But the children - O the children! -
  They who leaped to his caress,
And felt his arms about them,
  And his love and tenderness, -
Where - where will they find comfort
  As their tears fall like the rain,
And they swarm his face with kisses
  That he answers not again?

George W. Davids *(1835-1894)*

In 19th century America, poetry and journalism were sometimes surprisingly close companions as demonstrated by the work of the late 19th century Poughkeepsie journalist, George W. Davids.

As the child of a single mother, Davids left school at an early age to help support his family by selling his mother's pies and cakes to passengers on the Hudson River train line. As a young man, he was hired as a shipping clerk packing chairs at the Chichester Chair factory in Poughkeepsie. Davids seemed destined for a humble life.

But whenever the *Poughkeepsie Eagle* newspaper was delivered to the factory, there was George Davids waiting for the carrier "with a lot of little scraps of paper on which were written items of down town news, notes of happenings on the railroad or along the river, or bits of stray gossip that he had picked up among the workmen, or in going to and from his home, or in talk with his acquaintances."[1]

These "scraps of paper" found their way into the *Eagle* newspaper and were read with such interest that Davids decided to apply for the job of local news reporter. At his job interview, Davids boldly promised that if he could have the job, "he could furnish a column of news every day!" "But what if there isn't news enough to fill a column?" replied the skeptical editor.[2]

The editor need not have worried. Davids filled his column every day for many years with delightful tidbits gleaned from dozens and dozens of sources in every walk of life.

Davids remained the consummate journalist quite literally up to the time of his death. When first stricken with the disease which would eventually claim his life, his first instinct was to get his own story into the paper.

As soon as he recovered consciousness, he dictated an account of his illness and concluded with the sentence, "At 10 pm, Mr. Davids was resting easier." When his doctor observed that it was only 4 pm, Davids replied, "I know that well enough, but that is the way we do it in the newspaper business." [3]

At times, his vivid lists of news "scraps" turned his column into a prose poem of ordinary daily life in a late 19th century small town.

Signs of Spring

George W. Davids

(for the Poughkeepsie Daily Eagle*: March 4, 1882)*

A load of new churns painted sky blue passed through Main St. yesterday.

Windows were up and stove doors open yesterday.

Crowds of idlers on the streets daily, basking in the warm rays of the sun.

Easter cards are numerous, and the egg market is feverish.

Milliners are as busy as bees with "the latest style."

"To Lets" are decreasing in numbers rapidly.

Hoops, marbles and velocipedes begin to obstruct the walks.

Carpenters are busy, and men are seen going along the streets with long ladders.

A boy went down Main Street yesterday with a scapping net.

Arrivals at Eastman College are not as numerous as usual.

Little knots of people loaf about the Kaal Rock daily watching the river.

There is a falling off in the sale of buckwheat, and pancakes are disappearing.

Ducks are waddling about the edges of ponds and brooks.

Steamboat men are going north and south by rail.

Contracts are being made for the usual summer supply of ice.

Farmers are looking after farm labor.

Methodists are preparing for the annual Conference.

There has been a large increase in the number of baby carriages on the streets lately.

Politicians are discussing the probable results of town elections.

Advertisements of "spring styles" are beginning to flow in.

The wimmen folks are "rummaging" to see what they can find to trade away for tin pans, vases, etc. Hide your overcoat.

Sentimental people are beginnning to send "Spring, Spring, beautiful Spring" to the newspapers.

Tinkers are at work repairing gutters about the city.

Southern tomatoes are coming into the market.

Summer resort proprietors are engaging their help for the coming season.

Visits of drummers are becoming more numerous.

Wild ducks are coming up the Hudson.
The south sides of board fences begin to smoke.
Pitch, tar and oakum along the docks; and green paint, tarred rigging and old junk.
Clam fritters on the bill of fare.

Vassar College

For Vassar students of the late 19th and early 20th century, thinking in rhyme and meter seemed an astonishingly natural act, resulting in a surprising number of student poems and song lyrics for any and all campus occasions.

Perhaps creating poetry was an intoxicating release from the discipline of a demanding curriculum and the severity of campus rules. In his memoir of college life, college president Henry Noble MacCracken looked back fondly at this exhuberant era when student poetry was both vibrant and abundant.

But the world's complexity could not be kept from Vassar's door, and the innocence and intensity of campus poetic life became a quaint relic of the past. MacCracken noted with some sadness the changes 20th century life brought to Vassar: "The campus is older, wiser, more intellectual now; it is less spontaneous, joyous, creatively free. Its life is no longer centered in itself. The world, of labor and art, politics and economics, of international relations, has filled the mind. It is, however, rather impersonal. The old gaiety is gone and there is a lot to worry about." [1]

(from the Vassarion, *1891)*

The underclasses say
That a senior's life is play,
But any one who's tried it will that sentiment refute;
    For our duties grave are many,
    While repose - we haven't any,
And in vain we probe improbables, inscrutables we scrute.
    For our trials have begun
    When the rising bell has rung,
    We must scramble through our dressing,
    So as not to miss the blessing,
    Take a hasty cup of coffee and a roll;
    Dash off something deep and brainy,
    For the Vassar Miscellany,
    And speculate a little on the soul.
A rehearsal for a Philalethean play,
Then we help the young Omega on its way
Do some reading for a T. and M. debate,
And reason with the girl who stays up late;
    Run in something light and airy
    For a meeting literary
Of Alpha or of Beta (for on drama they have frowned).
    Then we hasten to seclude us
    In the great *tank melanudros*
(Though we always ask permission, so that no one will be drowned).
    Next devote some hasty glances
    To the national finances,
And ponder on the ills that money brings.
    We must practise in the choir,
    And take notes on the Messiah,
Then do a little on the travelling rings.
    Oh, the underclasses say
    That the senior's life is play,
But with duties we're distracted, and with labor we are spent,
    But 'tis balanced by the pleasure
    And the privilege we treasure
Of calling Sunday evening on our august president.

(from the Vassarion, *1892)*

Where are you going, my pretty maid?
To Vassar College, Sir, she said,
   Sir, she said,
   Sir, she said,
To Vassar College, Sir, she said.

May I go with you, my pretty maid?
'Tis a Female College, Sir, she said.
How may one enter there, my pretty maid?
Solely by intellect, Sir, she said.

What will you do there, my pretty maid?
Take an A.B., if I can, she said.
Then won't you marry me, my pretty maid?
Bachelors do not wed, Sir, she said.

What will you do then, my pretty maid?
I shall be Master of Arts, she said.
Then you won't marry me, my pretty maid?
You would be master of me, she said.

What will you do then, my pretty maid?
Try for a P.H.D., Sir, she said.
Then I won't marry you, my pretty maid!
Nobody asked you to, Sir, she said.
   Sir, she said,
   Sir, she said,
Nobody asked you to, Sir, she said.

(from the Vassarion*, 1895)*

Old Familiar Faces

Where are they gone, the old familiar faces?
We once had horse-cars, but they now have left us -
Left opportunely in a day of progress -
All, all are gone, the old familiar faces.

Poor patient horses, with their heavy burdens,
Always struggling onward; always slow, but faithful -
All, all are gone, the old familiar faces.

We were their friends, since nothing better offered,
Now, like ingrates, we leave our friends abruptly,
Forget the old: those dear familiar faces.

For trolley-cars have come, and horse cars have left us;
Their steeds are taken from us - all are departed;
All, all are gone, the old familiar faces.

(from the Vassarion*, 1902)*

Freshman Reception

Oh, dear, I am so very small,
The campus big, the buildings tall,
And home it is so far away,
I've met 600 girls today.

(from the Vassarion, *1906)*

An Agony of Tight Fits

Sue's room was exceedingly small,
So her books shelves she hung on the wall,
    For towels and soap
    In her closet she'd grope,
And she hadn't a bureau at all.

She didn't have space for a bed,
So she slept in a hammock instead,
    And she lived in a fright
    That twould fall in the night -
Though she slept very lightly, she said.

She kept all her waists in a box
That bruised her poor knuckles with knocks;
    And her knees grew quite sore
    Groveling round on the floor,
As she needs must to get out of her frocks.

When she asked a few friends (only three)
Her mother and sister to see,
    The guests had to come
    In parties of one,
And drink condensed milk in their tea.

One night, lying freezing in bed,
The book-shelves dropped down on her head;
    She fell amid groans
    And the breaking of bones,
And when she awoke she was dead!

(from the Vassarion, *1913)*

Securing Men for the Dance

(conversation between two Juniors overheard by a Freshman)

Is it your room-mate's brother -
   Or his uncle's cousin's chum?
No, my father's sister's office boy
   Has consented now to come.

Oh, how grand! Well, Glad and Madge
   Have advertised, they say;
I hope it works - That freak of mine
   Just let me know today.

The dreadful thing! Mine may back out,
   My dear, I'm worried blue
For fear he'll disappoint me - well, goodbye,
   Good luck to you!

Does Feminine Intellect Pay?

Wallace Irwin

Mihitabel Sullivan Scott
> When she journeyed from Vassar to stay
>> Looked calmly around
>> O'er the practical ground
> And asked in a logical way,
> "Does feminine intellect pay?"
But, being a maiden of mind,
> She started, in humbleness frank
>> Doing odd jobs and chores
>> For confectioners' stores
>> Till her salary grew,
>> And the first thing she knew
> She rose to responsible rank
> And they made her cashier of a bank.
>> *O say, little birdie, O say!*
> *Does feminine intellect pay?*
>> *Can a maiden so frail*
>> *Compete with the Male*
> *In practical work of the day?*

And while at her desk as cashier
> A burglar named Horrible Hank
>> Walked into the place
>> With a mask on his face
> Intent upon robbing a bank.
> (His criminal record was dank.)
But, ere he could call for his pals,
> The maiden seized Hank by a limb,
>> And, by using jiu-jits'
>> Soon reduced him to bits,
>> Then, spite of his squeals,
>> Hung him up by his heels
> (A trick she had learned in the gym.)
> And that was the finish of him.

O say, little birdie, O say!
Does feminine intellect pay?
   Is it true that she can
   Not compete with a man
 In the strenuous things of the day?

So, because of her coolness and nerve,
 To the President's son she was wed.
   She was easily boss,
   For when he was cross
 She spanked him and sent him to bed.
 (He was proud of her muscle, he said.)
And seventeen children she had
 Who grew to be hearty and hale.
   Some went to Vass-ar
   And some to Bryn Mawr
   To carry the fame
   Of the family name.
(But some, who were hopelessly Male,
Were silently packed off to Yale.)
   O say, little birdie, O say!
   Does feminine intellect pay?
     Has a maiden a mind
     Of the practical kind
   In the difficult tasks of the day?

    (1906)

Alta Mater

What gifts ask we at thy fair hands?
Thy love what grace imparts?
The will to dare, the hand to do,
Thy light within our hearts.

High, Mother, is thy heart,
As thy gray tower's height.
Strong, Mother, are thy hands,
Thy torch burns ever bright.

What gifts lay we at thy fair feet,
Since we are greatly blest?
Our strength, our hope, to bear thy light
Undimmed from east to west.

High, Mother, is thy heart,
As thy gray tower's height.
Strong, Mother, are thy hands,
Thy torch burns ever bright.

- Elizabeth Mason Heath, 1916

Light After Darkness

Harry V. Marr

Down below the river's flowing
  In a sun-kissed golden tide;
Up above the winds are blowing
  Soft along the mountain side;
But I feel no least temptation
  To stray either up or down; -
Here you find the explanation:
  The Vassar girls are back in town!

Through the summer sad and weary
  How I longed to fly away,
How I longed to tread the dreary
  Desert paths of far Cathay;
Even Newburgh in my madness
  Seemed a place my pain to drown: -
Ah, these words of glowing gladness -
  The Vassar girls are back in town!

Are they gone - I'd thread the courses
  Of the Ganges or the Nile;
Are they here - the wildest horses
  Cannot drag me half a mile!
Oh, the lonely long vacation,
  Heavy sorrow's heaviest crown;
Oh, the joyous exaltation
  With the Vassar girls in town!

(Poughkeepsie Daily Eagle: October 2, 1896)

Maria Mitchell *(1818-1889)*

Perhaps no other Vassar professor has been as deeply cherished by her students as Maria Mitchell, Vassar's first professor of Astronomy and director of the college observatory.

Mitchell first came to the world's attention after discovering a comet in 1847 while "sweeping the skies" over her Nantucket home. Her acceptance of a Vassar teaching position at age 47, meant the curtailment of much of her own scientific research. But Mitchell was a fierce advocate for the advancement of women, once noting, "I believe in women more than I do in Astronomy." Teaching became her passion and "her girls" (as she called them) her greatest endeavor. [1]

Mitchell was often compared to a brisk Nantucket breeze sweeping through the superheated rooms of college bureaucracy. In faculty politics, she refused to tolerate injustice and courageously complained when women professors were slighted or underpaid. But her only real interest was in her girls who plainly adored her for her remarkable blend of originality, enthusiasm and humor.

Her teaching of science emphasized independent thinking, patient observation, impeccable accuracy - and above all, free play of the imagination. Mitchell taught her students that Astronomy was "not all mathematics, nor all logic, but it is somewhat beauty and poetry." [2]

In her own "grand nights" of sweeping the moonlit Nantucket sky, Mitchell had imagined the Aurora Borealis as her companion and each meteor a messenger from the departed. A realm beyond what she called the "small cares" and the "littleness of our own interests" had opened before her. Her students were in awe of this empowerment through the stars, but took equal delight in her stories of foreign travel and scientific adventures beyond the narrow confines of campus life.

Mitchell's deep respect for her students was palpable. "I never look upon the mass of girls going into our dining room or chapel without feeling their nobility, the sovreignty of their pure spirit," she said. But it was her fondness for "her girls" and her great sense of fun that culminated in Mitchell's famous "Dome Parties" held each year in the observatory during the week before graduation. [3]

For this occasion, Mitchell converted the observatory dome into a festive hall with flowers and refreshments. But the highlight of the event was Mitchell's reading of her specially composed nonsense poetry, one poem written for each student. The girls were also invited to bring their own poems, and the evening ended each year with a rousing rendition of "Good Woman that She Was," a special song written by students for Professor Mitchell.

The Dome Party was a truly treasured event. One student some years later wrote,

> I have forgotten all I ever knew about the sun, moon and stars. I should not recognize the zenith if I met it face to face; and as for azimuth, I do not know whether it is the name of a place or a planet. But I never shall forget those little tables lighted with candles set about the great stone pillar in the dome, the bouquets and souvenirs at every plate, and the poetry, in that printlike handwriting, which Professor Mitchell made for every one of her girls. [4]

Mitchell's ability to "versify" can be traced to her Nantucket youth when a frozen harbor sometimes isolated her island home for weeks at a time. During such periods, Mitchell and her friends amused themselves by writing impromptu sonnets and memorizing 20 lines of poetry each day. One can imagine Mitchell even then, as a young Nantucket girl, writing poems to tease those she loved and reciting with passion her favorite poem, "The Spacious Firmament on High."

For Jenny Ricker

"Farewell, farewell, to thee, dear Jenny Ricker,"
Thus warbled a senior who started for home.
"The light of thy presence around me will flicker,
And show me the pathway wherever I roam."
Oh! ne'er till I saw thee, my dear Jenny Ricker,
Did I know what was winsome and peaceful and sweet.
No envy, no hatred, no quarrel, no bicker,
But love and good-will to all thou didst meet.

For Lizzie Adams
(Written the year the Astronomy textbook's author changed from God-fray to Chauvenet)

Lizzie Adams, bend your ear,
Bend it low, and list to hear.
Thy old lover, Godfray, sighs,
While he murmurs his good-byes.
Hear his parting words to thee:
"Adams, L., remember me."
When fishes swim the sky
When scorpion blinks his eye,
When a comet whizzes past,
When the moon's in shadow cast,
Be your North Star high or low,
Let one tear for Godfray flow.

For Jennie Patterson

Our senior class has such difficult names,
To fit them to rhymes a great genius claims.
We can rhyme upon Jones, upon Glenn and on King,
But to get one for Southworth's a difficult thing.
For Learned there's burn-ed and earn-ed and turn-ed,
For Broadbead I own I am slightly concern-ed,
For Easton, there's feast on,
For Warren, there's foreign,
But for Patterson no one as yet has found any,
So we'll drop the last name, and write rhymes to Jennie.

The Dome

Maria Mitchell

Within the room
That I call "home"
The wind may whistle around the Dome,
I let the wind whistle and pass
I shut my eyes to the frost on the pane
I shut my ears to the creaking vane
I shut my thoughts from the past and its pain,
I think of my girls soon women to be
Who daily bring peace and joy to me
Who watch the Bear whirl round in his lair,
Who get up too soon to look at the moon
Who go somewhat mad on the last Pleiad
Who seek to try on the sword of Orion
Who, lifting their hearts to the heavenly blue
Will do women's work for the good and the true
And as sisters or daughters or mothers or wives
 Will take the starlight into their lives.

Photo: Vassar College Observatory (1879)
(Special Collections, Vassar College Libraries)

Maria Mitchell
(or Good Woman that She Was)

Susanna C. Barton (Vassar Class of 1875)
Ella Gardner (Vassar Class of 1877)

(Sung to the tune of "Battle Hymn of the Republic")

We're singing for the glory of Maria Mitchell's name,
She lived at Vassar College, and you all do know the same.
She once did spy a comet and she thus was known to fame,
Good woman that she was.

(Chorus) Glory, glory Hallelujah!
Glory, glory Hallelujah!
Glory, glory, Hallelujah!
Good woman that she was.

In the cause of woman's suff - (e) - rage she shineth as a star,
And as President of Congress she is known from near and far,
For her 'xecutive ability and for her silver ha'r
Good woman that she was.
(Chorus)

Though as strong as the Rocky Mountain, she is gentle as a lamb,
And in her ways and manners she is peaceable and calm,
And our mental perturbations she sootheth like a balm,
Good woman that she am.
(Chorus)

Sing her praises, sing her praises, good woman that she were,
For though Pope says 'tis human, she is hardly known to err,
And from the path of virtue, she never strayed fur,
Good woman that she were.
(Chorus)

Sing her praises, sing her praises, good woman that she is,
For to give us joy and welcome, her chiefest pleasure 'tis,
Let her name be sung forever, till through space her praises whiz,
Good woman that she is.
(Chorus)

(The singing of this song became a traditional part of Professor Mitchell's annual dome party. When she heard it for the first time, Mitchell is said to have laughingly observed, "It is true I am not a wise woman, but I am a good one.")

Edna St. Vincent Millay
(1892-1950)

When 20 year old poet Edna St. Vincent Millay became a Vassar College freshman, it was the improbable realization of an improbable dream.

One of three daughters raised in Camden, Maine by an impoverished single mother, Millay's chances of attending college seemed slim. But in the summer of 1912, at the inn where her sister waitressed, Millay read her poem "Renascence" to a party of guests and staff. In the stunned audience was Caroline B. Dow, Dean of the YWCA National Training School, who was so taken with the obvious genius of this 19 year old girl that she offered to find sponsors willing to fund Millay's tuition at Vassar.

That same year, "Renascence" won fourth prize in a national poetry contest although several important critics and even the contest winners noted the prize obviously belonged to Millay. Critic Louis Untermeyer invited Millay to tea at his New York apartment and later remembered her powerful effect: "There was no other voice like hers in America. It was the sound of the ax on fresh wood." [1]

Although Smith College was also courting Millay, Vassar ultimately triumphed. The dazzled young woman from Camden, Maine wrote her mother: "I got a Vassar catalogue from someone today...I've had lots of fun looking up names, in that and in the Smith catalogue. ...In Vassar now there are four girls from Persia, two from Syria, two from Japan, one from Berlin, Germany...There isn't one 'furriner' in Smith. Lots of Maine girls go to Smith; very few to Vassar. I'd rather go to Vassar..." [2]

Millay arrived at Vassar (Class of 1917) as something of a celebrity, yet her adjustment was not easy. Her family was poor and her parents divorced. Her clothes were provided by her sponsors. Her high school preparation was spotty, and she had failed two entrance exams. In emotional and sexual development, she was four years older than the rest of her classmates. Millay wrote to a friend:

I hate this pink-and-gray college. If there had been a college in Alice in Wonderland it would be this college. Every morning when I awake I swear I say, 'Damn this pink-and-gray college!' It isn't on the Hudson. They lied to me. It isn't anywhere near the Hudson... They trust us with everything but men...a man is forbidden as if he were an apple... [3]

But Millay was quick to throw herself into Vassar life, writing to her mother a short time later:

...I'm getting so crazy about Vassar & so wrapped up in Vassar doings, that I don't have so much time as I used to have when I just liked it well enough...But oh, I love my college, my college, my college! Last night by the light of the moon we ran into a band of Seniors & a few others whom we knew out in the athletic circles on the bleachers, strumming the mandolin & singing, & we got boosted up along o' the rest & sang too & the moon shined bright as day & the warm wind blowed, & oh, didn't we love our college!... [4]

Her enthusiastic outpouring of songs, stories, poems, and plays for Vassar events of all kinds was calculated to insure that "the college will want to keep me" even when her daring hijinx made her the most notorious girl on campus. Vassar president Henry Noble MacCracken recalled one of his rather frequent disciplinary encounters with "Vincent" Millay:

In those days students could absent themselves whenever they pleased and just send in a sick excuse. I stopped [Millay] in the hall one of those times and said, "Vincent, you sent in a sick excuse at nine o'clock this morning and at ten o'clock I happened to look out the window of my office and you were trying to kick out the light in the chandelier on top of the Taylor Hall arch, which seemed a rather lively exercise for someone so taken with illness. She looked very solemnly at me and said to me, 'Prexy, at the moment of your class, I was in pain with a poem.' What could you do with a girl like that? [5]

Millay was also well known at Vassar for her powerful physical allure. She was described as having a luminous, even magical presence with her pale skin and strawberry red hair. And with the instincts of a fine actress, she had already taken pains to cultivate an irresistably rich and vibrant voice which she would use throughout her life to mesmerize audiences at her popular poetry readings. At Vassar, she bewitched her classmates (and some of the faculty) with her wit and her wildness, casually seducing those who interested her. Only six years after her graduation from Vassar (a graduaton she almost missed after being suspended for staying out all night), Millay became the first woman to win a Pulitzer Prize for poetry.

Why Did I Ever Come to This Place?

(an expedition in untrammelled verse)

Sometimes
When the eight o'clock bell rings,
And the maids,
In a long, black, frantic line,
Scurry from the dining-room
Like rats
From a doomed ship,
Nor will any of them catch my eye
(Though I have been waiting
As patient as a farmer's wife
Since dawn)
I say to myself,
Or to any who cares to listen,
That college is a bore,
And that woman's place
Is in the home.
And again,
When the chapel chimes,
Forgetting that it is TOWN SUNDAY,
(or uninformed)
Ding,
That is to say, "peal",
For quite some time,
As blithe
And inexorable,
And out of tune,
As anyody else in a bath-tub,
(Or as foolishly complacent
As a football player
Who runs in the wrong direction
And scores a goal
For the other side)
I turn in bed,
And glare at the plaster, which is scarred
By generations of thumb-tacks,

For whose insertion I,
As guiltless
As is a Freshman of knowledge,
Do semi-annually
Settle,
And I say to myself,
Or to the servant who comes in just then
To empty the wastebasket,
That college
Is the misapprehension
Of a June-bug mind,
And that woman's place
Is in the home.
And always
When with some youth,
Whom I do not love,
But might,
In the proper environment,
I have trudged for hours,
Pointing out the Library
And the Art Building,
Over and over,
(For the parlors
Are full of parents,
And five room-mates
Are an insufficient chaperone)
Always
I say to myself,
Or to the night-watchman,
Who does not care,
That I wish I were happily married
To a dyspeptic widower
With six small children,
And that higher education for women
Is as paradoxical a quantity
As prohibition at election time,
And that woman's place
Is in the home.

E. St. V. M., 1917

Riverview Academy

Poughkeepsie's Riverview Academy was first established in 1836 as the Poughkeepsie Collegiate School, magnificently located on College Hill high above the village. In 1867, the school changed its name to Riverview Military Academy and moved to a new but also spectacular setting on a bluff overlooking the Hudson River. Here boys were promised "robust physiques" and the development of their "manly side" through "military drill, out-door sports, well-bred society and earnest study."[1]

Riverview closed in 1916 and was almost entirely demolished by the City of Poughkeepsie in 1921. One of the Academy's annex buildings survived to become the Lincoln Community Center, a neighborhood social services facility operated by Vassar College. Arson destroyed the Lincoln Center campus in 1979, and today the bluff overlooking the Hudson River is home to the fields of the Lincoln Park Soccer Club.

The Riverview Academy's annual February "Hop" was wildly anticipated among local youths, and created no small amount of wistful nostalgia among the evening's adult chaperones. Details of the evening were printed in local newspapers for days following the event.

The Riverview dance that inspired the following poem is described in the *Poughkeepsie Daily Eagle* (February 25, 1897):

> *The young girls of Poughkeepsie as well as the students of Riverview have been looking forward to the annual Riverview hop for weeks. It is the one great social event of the season for them; they date from the Riverview hop and during the rest of the year you will hear them refer to things as having occurred before or after the 24th of February...*

> *The scheme of decoration in the drill hall this year is entirely different from that which has prevailed for a number of years past. The 'corners' devoted to special sports, which were wont to be museums of baseball or football paraphenalia, boxing gloves, tennis rackets, etc. are absent this year as are also the amateur photographic displays, the college colors and the musical instruments. 'Patriotic' seems to*

be the word to describe the big drill hall as it appeared on Wednesday night. The walls were a mass of warm color, the effect being produced chiefly by flags. Conspicuous were two Hudson River championship trophies won by the school in baseball...

At the end of the hall over the door leading to the armory were the letters R.M.A. [Riverview Military Academy] in incandescent electric lights on a background of evergreens. These lights were the work of two of the students Godinez and J.L. Curtis who are excellent electricians. They did the wiring and arranged an ingenious current so that the lights would flash out and die out every few seconds. The motor they had to use in making and breaking the circuit was too rapid, and they rigged up a bicycle wheel to reduce the speed...

Palms and potted plants were in every available place where they would not interfere with dancing. Off the dining room the classes of 97 and 98 had very comfortable and cosy parlors, fitted up after a struggle with curtain poles, etc. and containing luxurious sofas and easy chairs and nooks for quiet flirtations. They were very popular during the evening...Down in the ball room, or drill hall, Scofield's Orchestra was stationed on a platform in the northwest corner, so that the dining room could also be used for dancing....Supper was served by Smith Brothers in the large school room, which was filled in relays. When the bugle sounded tattoo at 1 o'clock, most of the adieux had been said, but a long line of people remained in the halls and parlors waiting for their carriages. There will be plenty of young people in Poughkeepsie today too tired to get their lessons, but what are lessons to such a good time as that? One can't be young always.

The Riverview Hop

L. James (For the Poughkeepsie Daily Eagle, *March 3, 1897)*

Once more the military school,
　　Its drudgery did stop,
To let the scholars celebrate
　　Their semi-annual hop.

The invitations had been sent,
　　South, east, and west and north,
With hopes that all the girls would come
　　Upon the twenty-fourth.

And as the military boy
　　Stands high in female mind,
The girls who staid at home that night
　　Would be a job to find.

Oh what delerious joy it is,
　　When one receives the chance, -
To guide a blushing maiden through
　　The giddy whirling dance.

Reeds, polkas, two-steps and the waltz,
　　Were danced with animation,
While parents watched their youthful ones
　　And smiled in approbation.

Perhaps when intermission came,
　　The loving ones went strolling
Throughout the dimly-lighted halls,
　　Their love for each other extolling.

Until some mischievous cadet,
　　Who like a prying elf,
Breaks up their little tete a tete, -
　　I've been there, boys, myself.

But every one enjoyed themselves,
　　Which fills me with delight;
(I heard the carriages go home
　　At two o'clock at night.)

Poughkeepsie Regatta

Almost every year from 1895 to 1949, Poughkeepsie was host to one of the most prestigious and anticipated events in all of college sports, the Intercollegiate Rowing Association (IRA) Regatta held annually in June. This famous winner-take-all, roughly 20 minute race took place on what many considered the finest four mile rowing course in the country, and for decades, Poughkeepsie was known as the "rowing capital" of the United States.

Crowd estimates varied from 30,000 to 50,000 to 100,000 spectators, perched with their picnic baskets and pennants on every available rooftop and rock. The best views, however, were from bleachers set up on board a special flat bed "observation train" that chugged slowly along at the river's edge as the race was run.

Still other spectators crowded out on to the river itself in private yachts, fishing boats and chartered ships, some firing cannons from their decks as the crews passed by. Cornell rower Mark Odell recollected that in the 1897 regatta:

> The last mile was a flotilla of yachts, which kept up the most infernal pandemonium you can imagine. Not a word could we hear of our coxswain's orders. Cannons were going off right above our heads which made it feel as though the top of the skull was coming off at each shot, whistles of the most infernal screeching power went off in our ears. 'Hell was let loose,' as they say in the classics.[1]

A few weeks prior to race day, crews, coaches, bookmakers, and reporters began trickling in to Poughkeepsie as each team began its practice regimen and took up temporary quarters in donated riverfront mansions or boarding houses.

Photo: Stanford University Crew
(Library of Congress Prints and Photographs Division)

Although there were only three founding members (Columbia, Cornell and the University of Pennsylvania) when the Intercollegiate Rowing Association formed in 1895, the event grew over the years to a much larger invitational including Harvard, Yale, Princeton, Stanford, Navy, Dartmouth, University of California, University of Washington, University of Wisconsin, and Syracuse University. The breadth of the Hudson River at Poughkeepsie easily accomodated the growing field.

As race day approached, buildings all over Poughkeepsie were draped in gay bunting and banners displaying rival college colors. Special trains carrying hundreds of alumni and rowing fans from across the nation arrived at nearby stations. Betting was vigorous. A steady stream of "college boys" flowed in and out of the billiard room at the Nelson House Hotel where wagering began early on race day morning. Men came to the race wearing hat bands in their favorite team's colors, while ladies in their summer white shirtwaists waved a sea of white hankies from the shore.

In 1896, a journalist captured the spectacle's sparkling mix of summertime fizziness and high drama:

> Men and women, thousands upon thousands of them in gayest colors on mountain and rocks, the green of the trees, the granite's gray, the sparkling of rippled water, the glory of a summer sun, scores of yachts decked like birds and 32 perfect physical men to do battle with all the pluck and strength that God gave them and the skill that men could teach - all these were there.[2]

In 1950, the Regatta left Poughkeepsie forever when the sport abandoned the punishing athletic standards required by a four mile long race on a tidal river. Today's Intercollegiate Regatta is held in a series of qualifying heats on a 1.2 mile course in Camden, New Jersey's Cooper River.

The following four poems celebrate one of the most famous college crew races of all time - the Poughkeepsie Regatta of June, 1897. That year, as race time approached, the official "yells" of each college could be heard spontaneously ringing out all over Poughkeepsie. Cornell's yell ("Cornell! Cornell! I yell, yell, yell, Cornell!") was created by Cornell crew fans in 1875 as a pun on the Yale glee club tune, "As Freshmen first we came to Yale/Eli, Eli, Eli Yale." But since those famous Yale-Harvard-Cornell crew matches on Saratoga Lake in 1875 and 1876, Cornell had been waiting more than twenty years for a varsity rematch with their disdainful powerhouse rivals, Yale and Harvard.

The rematch took place at the Poughkeepsie Regatta of 1897, and Cornell came with something to prove. Pundits and bookmakers, who gave Cornell virtually no chance of winning, failed to realize that Cornell viewed the race as nothing less than the symbolic assertion of their school's right to belong in the ivy league. As the race was about to begin, the ominous final words of the Cornell coach to his crew were, "Either you're Cornell or you're nothing." [3]

The three length victory by Cornell was an utterly astonishing sports upset that one newspaper called the "triumph of brain and soul and spirit over brute muscle." Cornell's unusual technique (previously mocked as the "git thar" stroke) was now declared pure American genius.

After weeks of intense training, regatta night was traditionally a time to cut loose in wild celebration. The Cornell crew's victory night in 1897

involved, as one local paper put it, "taking on more beer than was good for them" - but behavior was generally orderly. [4]

Hundreds of fans doing the "Cornell Yell" attended an impromptu serenade of Cornell's crew coach, then paraded through Poughkeepsie's streets until well after midnight waving Cornell banners, shooting off fireworks and blowing tin horns. Loyal Cornell alumni who bet on dear old alma mater to win certainly left Dutchess County richer than when they came.

Photo: Intercollegiate Race at Poughkeepsie (1914)
(Library of Congress)

A Review and a Forecast

The Hudson's waves to sleep had gone,
    The sun had said "Good Night,"
The mountains reared their lofty heads,
    And wondered at the sight:
For the valley down below them
    Reechoed Eli's knell
As from a thousand throats there came
    Cornell, I yell, Cornell.

The voices of the crowd were hushed,
    And each one gazed intent,
As eight and forty stalwart arms
    Upon their oars were bent.
And when the pistol shot was fired,
    There rose a mighty yell,
Yet clear above them all was heard,
    Cornell, I yell, Cornell.

They're off and Harvard's crimson oars
    Triumphant led the way,
And close upon their rippling course
    The sons of Eli lay.
And last of all the crews there came,
    Yet rowing strong and well,
The sturdy eight that heard the cry,
    Cornell, I yell, Cornell.

"Aye, pull ye well, ye men in blue,
    You have good cause to fear,
We've waited twenty years or more,
    And now our time is here."
So thought the crowd, whose long huzzah
    No power on earth could quell,
And as we passed old Yale they cried,
    Cornell, I yell, Cornell.

In vain they sprint, and all in vain
    Their frantic coxswain cries,

For there across the finish line
  Our crew exultant lies.
As from a thousand gladdened throats,
  A cry triumphant fell,
And the mountain side hurled back the cry,
  Cornell, I yell, Cornell.
                    - anonymous Cornell student

Photo: Cornell Crew at Poughkeepsie (1897)
(New York Public Library)

Gold

"Well, well, well! After twenty years!
What did we do! The same old thing."
So we sang with merry voices in gay Poughkeepsie town,
And the band played Alma Mater, as the sun was going down;
And the sky was blue no longer, but was streaked with red and white,
While we shouted loud the promise of 'A Hot Old Town To-night.'
We had cashed in every voucher till our pockets could not hold
The ripe, rich yellow harvest of Yale and Harvard Gold.

Refrain:
Oh, the gold! Oh, the gold!
Oh, the bright New Haven gold!
Just as free as 'twas of old,
When the day grew dark and cold
For Eli's scions bold
As they bit the dusty mould,
And our gallant 'Farmers' rolled
In the bright New Haven gold,
Gold, gold, gold, gold, gold, gold, gold!

Since that pleasant summer evening in the turbid Hudson town,
When we showed our friends from Harvard how to throw old Eli down,
We've been constantly admonished by a friendly multitude
To appear before the public in a novel attitude:
They believed we ought to quibble, and to bicker and to fight,
Just because at old Poughkeepsie there was nothing else in sight.

But at last it is decided in the grand old Cornell way, -
We will row with anybody, anywhere, and any day;
We will travel to New London, not quite penniless, I trust,
And though gambling is immoral, if you must, of course you must.
If to shake it in our faces both Yale and Harvard join,
It will be our sacred duty to relieve them of their coin.

- anonymous Cornell student

A Timely Warning

Harry V. Maar

You students who now daily dip
    The bending oar in the tide,
Here let me offer you a tip
    As friend, philosopher and guide:
Now when the race is fairly won,
    And forth there bursts the echoing cheer,
There is a thing you'd better shun -
    To wit: Poughkeepsie beer!

Poughkeepsie beer! A potent brew;
    A cunning brew; a brew of might!
And one which a very few
    Can stand against half a night;
A heady brew in old days planned,
    Passed down to us through many a year,
A brew from M.V.'s master hand -
    Beware Poughkeepsie's beer!

There's river water filtered nice,
    Apolinaris in good store,
And ginger pop and tea with ice,
    And lemonade, and many more.
But steins and schooners you must shun,
    No man may touch them without fear;
If tempted turn thy face and run -
    Oh, strong Poughkeepsie beer!

A College Rowing Song

Firmly catch and swiftly pull
    The polished, pliant, springing oar
While muscles swell out full,
    And the heart throbs more and more;
Up the stream with rhythmic swing
    Sweet as music in the night,
While the straining rowlocks ring,
    And the blood leaps in delight,
            With the old, long stroke,
            With the old, long stroke,
That shall bring us in as winners, boys,
            At last.

Soon will come that burning day
    When the pistol shot will crack,
And our boat will rush away,
    As we strain each brawny back,
Pulling as we ne'er before
    Pulled, yet still with form and grace, -
Flying down to win the race,
            With the old, long stroke,
            With the old, long stroke,
That shall bring us in as winners, boys,
            At last.

So when the rowing here is done,
    And we seek the sea of life,
Where our prizes must be won
    In a swifter stream of strife,
We shall labor as of yore,
    Grim resolve on every face,
Bending bravely to the oar,
    Pulling hard to win the race,
            With the old, long stroke,
            With the old, long stroke,
That shall bring us in as winners, boys,
            At last.

-W.J.H., Cornell

In his late 19th century poem "Rhinebeck the Beautiful," piano and organ dealer Joseph T. Hammick unwittingly created a rather unique record of Rhinebeck's commercial history. In a preface to the 1897 third edition of his lengthy poem, Hammick explained that his goal had been nothing short of capturing both the beauty of the village and its entire business life in the highly concentrated form verse demands.

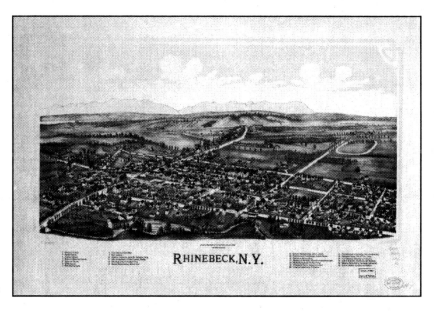

He considered it an "immense undertaking," and certainly, he risked offending a neighbor or colleague accidentally left out of the poem (the third edition was created to add descriptions of previously omitted "dressmakers and farmers").

Beyond giving his neighbors the thrill of seeing their names in rhyme and print, Hammick's poem is a classic example of small town boosterism that also delivered a message of warning: Unless Rhinebeck citizens embraced commercial "progress," they would be left behind in an increasingly industrialized world.

Illustration: Map of Rhinebeck (1890)
(Library of Congress Geography and Maps Division)

Rhinebeck, the Beautiful

J.T. Hammick

Beautiful Rhinbeck, not down by the sea,
But up along the Hudson, there long known to be;
In this beautiful valley of the Hudson, most grand,
Is Rhinebeck, this Eden, this glorious land.

Surrounded with grandeur with beauties untold,
These mountains, this river, its glories behold!
See our beautiful Maples, adorning each street,
Their foliage so lovely, so balmy and sweet;
Our lawns seem so glorious, these streets, just behold!
Like fine polished marble, like boulevards old...

Grand Rhinebeck, most lovely of all we behold!
More restful than any other place, we are told
Surrounded by Baronial estates, just as grand
As found in Europe or in any foreign land...

Our Rhinebeck location, none other than fine,
In the march of improvement, let Rhinebeck men join,
With the rush of great people, let us join in the throng,
Raise banners of glory, build grandly and strong!

Make Rhinebeck a city, whose fame shall extend
Beyond the great Rockies, yet to the world's end!
For its most charming beauties, its enterprise great,
Grown from village to city, in this great New York state...

Rhinebeck has its merchants, of most every kind,
Some have dry goods with crockery combined,
Anything you wish for, please to them just tell,
They've whatever you want, will most gladly sell.

Should you wish for fine goods, please then just enquire
For Bates, Coon or Ackert get all you desire.
Of Bates get your satins, of Coon get your shoes,
Of Ackert buy coats or whatever you choose...

Two drug stores in Rhinebeck with drugs all abound,
Can supply needed doses when sick folks are found:
Go to Baker's or to Feroe's and you will find
All medicines for the body, kind words for the mind.

Secor has fine marble, he keeps it on hand,
In readiness to furnish at each ones command;
In memory of loved ones, you'll place at the head,
This undying token, a monument for the dead...

Tremper and Asher with assortment quite great,
Will attend to your wants not long make you wait;
For oil that will burn or for nails that will hold,
Buildings well nailed till their builders grow old.

Carpenters we've many good workmen in town,
Bookstaver, Stickle, Decker, Ackert and Brown;
All together could build quite a city you see,
Could they all work together, and always agree...

Hammick has a full stock of Pianos, organs too.
Terms easy, rent or purchase for old ones, or new,
Will tune or repair them do most anything,
Make old pianos talk, and like new pianos sing...

Our noble free library with its thousands of books,
At our Starr Institute, most grand to us looks!
With magazines and papers, can every one read,
Donated by Mrs. Miller, what a memorial indeed!

Her name we'll remember when e'er there we go,
And draw books from this library, as years onward flow,
We'll hold her name sacred, with reverence and pride,
Her name will shine greatly, till the people have died...

At Toneu's or at Birch's buy pipes, cakes and candy.
Fine tobacco, cigars and matches there handy,
There's Snyder way uptown a nice store doth keep,
Has an assortment of groceries he'll sell to you cheap.

Riley has a market keeping all kinds of fish,

When Lent comes we've something to put on our dish!
Always at Riley's fresh fruit on his stand,
Oranges and bananas from a far away land...

Seems the men of our town are here for a rest,
They wish not by electric bells be distressed;
No railroad for Rhinebeck, no! no!! ten times no!
No improvements to build up Rhinebeck shall go.

We'll sleep on, all quiet, while other towns grow great,
We'll stave off improvements, all quiet, we'll wait,
Till we sink out of sight, in the grand rush we'll find,
In the march of improvement we're left far behind...

We've quiet been sleeping now awaken with fright!
Hear factory bells ringing, see electric cars light!
Our streets like a city, such enterprise great,
All set in commotion, while we were sleeping late...

These new enterprises, like mushrooms soon grew,
Men came from abroad, new life put them through,
Of enterprise, gentlemen, don't be afraid!
Then lots won't be selling for one-quarter you paid!...

Dutchess County
Courthouse *(1809-1902)*

Throughout the 19th century, the unique power of poetic language was commonly summoned to express both the joyfulness and the grandeur of a community's most important civic events. But on rarer occasions, it also became a vehicle for angry protest and an indicator of community divisions.

The following poem, written under the pen name of "Carl Keepsie," expresses the mix of anger and sad dismay felt by many at the demolition of Dutchess County's fourth courthouse - constructed by 1809 and torn down in 1902 to make way for the current county courthouse.

Those in favor of saving the building thought it both handsome and quite refined with its charming cupola and aura of solid Dutch colonial antiquity. But while some called it Dutchess County's version of Faneuill Hall in Boston or Independence Hall in Philadelphia, others thought it reminiscent of "an old fashioned barn. The bell on top of it seems to have been put there to call in the hands from the fields." [1]

When lawyers interested more in functionality than in heritage preservation united to condemn the building as a disgrace, its fate was sealed. During demolition, dynamite was required to topple the building's monumental limestone walls. Remnants were used as fill in the construction of a new Poughkeepsie street named Dwight.

The Vandal

Once upon a winter morning, as I watched the icy dawning,
As it flooded street and city with its rich and glittering store -
Suddenly I heard a crashing, that was dint of cruel smashing
Sent the chills all through me dashing, as I'd never known before.
"Tis a hurricane," I muttered, as it smote me with its roar -
"Or a storm from the mountains - Only this and nothing more."

Then I saw some strangers smiling, as if idle hours beguiling,
While the fragments still were piling, bits of ceiling, sill and door,
"Why this levity?" I muttered, but they not a sentence uttered -
Just then, wailing, fell a floor.
Tis some outrage here beginning, shall I stop this brutal sinning?
Shall I smite these ghouls for grinning? "Stop! Stop! there, I implore."
Quoth an echo - "Nevermore."

Then I stood to watch the tearing, while the strangers fell to swearing,
Not for glass or stairway caring - moaned the ripping of the floor -
When out stepped an angry vandal, with a visage grim as scandal,
Like a monster washed ashore.
"Pray," I shouted, "cease this breaking, give our hearts surcease from aching,
Let our souls escape this quaking, and tell us, what's this for?"
Roared the vandal - "Nevermore."

Then with melancholy seeming, came the thought, "I must be dreaming.
'Tis a nightmare here that's gleaming; wake me! wake me! I implore."
But the vandal stood there glaring, for still further spoil preparing,
Like a half surfeited boar.
"Why pursue this awful wreck, sir? care you not for architecture?
Of your plan give some conjecture, and your impudence deplore!"
Roared the vandal - "Nevermore."

Then I listened to the falling of the timbers, grim, appalling,
While from out the crashing tumult caught I echoes of the yore,
Every beam reluctant yielded, as from blows it would be shielded -
And the old bell, - sadly passed it forth a mighty roar.
Then came voices, weird and pleading, as from hearts in sorrow bleeding,
"Will their cries receive no heeding? pray, spare them, I implore."
Screamed the vandal "Nevermore."

Then I turned, with anger leaping at the sight of cruel heaping
   In a blasted pile our treasure of the honest days of yore,
"Vandal man," I cried, "who art thou? tell us what you mean to do now?
   Or begone, begone, I tell you, to your own spoils seeking shore.
Take thy clutch from off our court house, take thy footsteps from our door."
     Hissed the vandal - "Nevermore."

Then I straightaway fell to weeping, o'er destruction so allsweeping,
   And for memories in our keeping, we shall never cherish more,
And I watched the building falling, and I heard the voices calling,
   Of our forefathers - appalling - out against the vandal's roar.
And the monster still is swinging high his axe and bringing
      Down the court house, loved so well in days of yore
      And will leave us - Nevermore.
                - Carl Keepsie
       (With profound apologies to the immortal Poe.)

John Jay Chapman (1862-1933)

The brilliant provocateur and cultural critic, John Jay Chapman, became part of Dutchess County history in 1898 when he married Elizabeth Winthrop Chanler, the eldest surviving sister among the famed "Astor orphans" of Rokeby. Fortunately, Chapman was unfazed by the volatile and sometimes eccentric doings of his wife's famous siblings. He once observed dryly, "There is always one Chanler in the newspapers. The Chanler theme dies in the bassoons and is dropped in the pathetic drum solo - but hark the flute!" [1]

The Astor fortune was more problematic. As a zealous social reformer, Chapman was leery of money's seductive power and reminded his wife, "The first thing you know we'll be drowned in possessions and then by thinking of our horse's health...Let's keep the New Testament before us. The losing of wrath is to be feared." [2]

With financial security, however, Chapman was able to abandon his dull law practice to courageously bear witness against the cruelty, greed and moral corruption of America's robber baron age. His true career became that of independent public scholar - writing, lecturing and agitating for reforms outside the narrow confines of academia and even outside the confines of a single discipline.

His remarkable intellectual range (demonstrated in 25 books including plays, poems, translations, essays, biography, and literary criticism) has made him difficult to categorize. Despite a few impressive champions like critic Edmund Wilson (who considered Chapman the best letter writer America ever produced and the best writer on literature of his generation), Chapman's work remains little known today.

Chapman's superb professional intellect was matched only by the darkness of his personal passions. In a famous incident during his days at Harvard Law School, Chapman beat a man whom he incorrectly thought had insulted his dear friend, Minna Timmins. In chillingly calm prose, Chapman later described what happened after the beating:

The next thing I remember is returning late at night to my room. At that time I was rooming alone in a desolate side-street in Cambridge. It was a small, horrid little room. I sat down. There was a hard-coal fire burning brightly. I took off my coat and waist coat, wrapped a pair of suspenders tightly on my left forearm above the wrist, plunged the left hand deep in the blaze and held it down with my right hand for some minutes. When I took it out, the charred knuckles and finger bones were exposed. I said to myself, "This will never do!" I took an old coat, wrapped it about my left hand and arm, slipped my right arm into an overcoat, held the coat about me, and started for Boston in the horsecars. On arriving at Massachusetts General Hospital, I showed the trouble to the surgeon, was put under ether, and the next morning waked up without the hand and very calm in my spirits...I took no interest in the scandal which my two atrocious acts must have occasioned. [3]

As a result of this act of self-mutilation, Chapman found that life "opened" before him. He acknowledged his passionate love for Minna Timmins (whom he soon married), and threw himself into the role of writer, critic and "practical agitator" for social reform. When his beloved Minna died shortly after the birth of their third son, Chapman married family friend Elizabeth Chanler and continued delivering provocative cultural critiques and leading government reform crusades.

Yet his efforts felt, in his words,"like Atlas lifting the entire universe." In 1900, Chapman broke down in the middle of a lecture appearance and retreated to a tower bedroom at the Chanler's Rokeby estate where he remained bedridden in total darkness for the next year. During his subsequent slow recovery abroad, one of Chapman's sons accidentally drowned. The shock of this loss was so intense that Chapman suddenly and somewhat mysteriously regained full use of his legs.

In 1914, Chapman's son Victor, then an architecture student in Paris, enlisted in the French Foreign Legion and in 1916, became the first American flier shot down and killed over German enemy lines. In the week following his death, Victor Chapman captured the imagination of the entire world and became a revered international symbol of American fearlessness and self-sacrifice.

Chapman spent much of the last decades of his life at Sylvania, the Barrytown estate he and his wife Elizabeth created in 1905 adjacent to Rokeby. His impulsive gestures of political and moral outrage were at times still stunningly moving, but for the most part, he had become what he referred to as "a soul crushed by democracy." Chapman's poems, collected in 1919, are notable for their occasionally striking metaphors and the haunting emotional power lurking under a deceptively calm surface.

May, 1917

John Jay Chapman

The earth is damp: in everything
   I taste the bitter breath of pallid spring.
Hark! In the air a fanning sound,
Like distant beehives. -Ah, the woods awake;
And finding they are naked, cast around
A mist, like that which trembles on the lake.
    The forest murmurs, shudders, sings
    On pipes and strings,
    With harp and flute;
    And then turns coy,
    As if ashamed to show its joy,
And in a flush of happiness grows mute.

Alas, the spring! Ah, liquid light,
Your vistas of transparent green
Fall on my spirit like a blight.
The tapestries you hang on high
Are like a pageant to a sick man's eye,
    Or sights in fever seen.
Behind your bowers and your blooms
Volcanic desolation looms;
    Your life doth death express;
Each leaf proclaims a blackened waste,
Each tree, some paradise defaced,
    Each bud, a wilderness.
And all your lisping notes are drowned
By one deep murmur underground
    That tells us joy is fled,
    Love, innocence, the heart's desire,
    The flashing of Apollo's lyre, -
Beauty herself is dead.

In all the valleys of the earth, -
Save for the dead, - no wreath is hung.
    Long, long ago the sounds of mirth
    Died on man's tongue.

And life a broken lute;
Time's pendulum has stopped: a throng
Of huddling moments press along
  Untimed, in mad pursuit,
And into days and months are whirled,
As in a dream of pain.

Chaos has wrecked the outer world,
Chaos invades the brain.
The sounds, the sights, the scents of spring
Awake that sullen suffering
Which opium soothes in vain, -
Like the sad dawn of dread relief
That tells the greatness of his grief
To him that is insane.

Would I had perished with the past!
    Would I had shared that fate
    Of those who heard the trumpet-call
    And rode upon the blast,-
    Who stopped not to debate,
      Nor strove to save,
    But giving life, gave all,
Casting their manhood as a man might cast
    A rose upon a grave.
Would that like them beneath the sod I lay,
    Beneath the glistening grass,
    Beneath the flood of things that come, and pass,
      Beckon, and shine and fade away.

Autumn Dews

John Jay Chapman

Throw open the shutters, it's seven o'clock!
   And impertinent crows take their flight at the shock;
  Then dropping their breakfast, they scoff as they pass
  O'er the blanket of dew that lies white on the grass.

The mists from the shoulders of hillsides are slipping;
The low Autumn sun burns the dew-drops alive;
   And barberry-bushes with rubies are dripping,
   And gardners are heaping dead leaves by the drive.

O haste to the forest! - the forest whose fingers
Are clasping dank, green, little jewels of lawn:
   Perhaps in some shadowy clearing still lingers
   The track of the hare and the flame of the dawn.

To a Dog

John Jay Chapman

Past happiness dissolves. It fades away,
    Ghost-like, in that dim attic of the mind
To which the dreams of childhood are consigned.
Here, withered garlands hang in slow decay,
And trophies glimmer in the dying ray
Of stars that once with heavenly glory shined.
But you, old friend, are you still left behind
To tell the nearness of life's yesterday?
Ah, boon companion of my vanished boy,
For you he lives; in every sylvan walk
He waits; and you expect him everywhere.
How would you stir, what cries, what bounds of joy,
If but his voice were heard in casual talk,
If but his footstep sounded on the stair!

Retrospection

John Jay Chapman

When we all lived together
    In the farm among the hills,
And the early summer weather
    Had flushed the little rills;

And Jack and Tom were playing
    Beside the open door,
And little Jane was maying
    On the slanting meadow floor;

And mother clipped the trellis,
    And father read his book
By the little attic window, -
    So close above the brook:

How little did we reckon
    Of ghosts that flit and pass,
Of fates that nod and beckon
    In the shadows on the grass;

Of beauty soon deflowered,
    Engulfed, and borne away, -
And youth that sinks devoured
    In the chasm of a day!

Courageous and undaunted,
    As in a golden haze
We lived a life enchanted,
    Nor stopped to count the days.

We that were in the story
    Saw not the magic light,
The pathos, and the glory
    That shines on me to-night.

The Moral of History

John Jay Chapman

All is one issue, every skirmish tells,
    And war is but the picture in the story;
The plot's below: from time to time upwells
    A scene of blood and glory,
That makes us understand the allegory, -
A lurid flash of verse, - and at its close
    Recurring, undiscipherable prose.

The Hudson

John Jay Chapman

Bathed in a dying light
    The far out-stretching valley lies
Beneath the mingling veils of day and night;
    Fruit trees and gardens, woodland and champaign,
Paths, lawns and labyrinths - a Paradise.
    The mountains darken, and the clear
    Black waters at their base appear
Sending a last bright message from the skies.
It floods the all-but-lost Elysian plain
    Where knoll and bower
    Shimmer and peep, till the soft twilight hour, -
To add the magic of a new surprise, -
Washes them into silver gloom again.

Heroes

John Jay Chapman

I see them hasting toward the light
    Where war's dim watchfires glow;
The stars that burn in Europe's night
    Conduct them to the foe.

As when a flower feels the sun
    And opens to the sky,
Knowing their dream has just begun
    They hasten forth to die.

Be it the mystery of love -
    Be it the might of Truth -
Some wisdom that we know not of
    Controls the heart of youth.

All that philosophy might guess
    These children of the light
In one right act of death compress,
    Then vanish from our sight.

Like meteors on a midnight sky
    They break - so clear, so brief -
Their glory lingers on the eye
    And leaves no room for grief.

And when to joy old sorrows turn,
    To spring war's winter long,
Their blood in every heart will burn
    Their life in every song.

Margaret Chanler Aldrich
(1870-1963)

Orphaned at age five, Margaret Chanler Aldrich (along with her ten brothers and sisters) grew up in the care of her father's spinster cousin at the family's Barrytown estate of Rokeby. As an adult, Margaret Chanler Aldrich purchased the Rokeby shares of her siblings, the flamboyant and fascinating "Astor orphans," to become sole owner of Rokeby where she presided as family matriarch until her death at age 92.

Throughout her life, she remained devoted to performing the meticulous community service she felt was incumbent upon her as a "river family" society matron. Biographer Lately Thomas describes Margaret Chanler Aldrich's stalwart dedication to instilling this same sense of responsiblity among her nieces who were assigned "to sweep out the church at Red Hook, supply the altar with flowers, sell tickets for the church bazaar (and then attend and patronize the booths), entertain the rector at tea, help organize the annual party at St. Margaret's Home, appear at village funerals, trim the Rokeby Christmas tree, and organize barn dances for all the retainers and neighbors. Only through loyalty to God, church, home, and country, could the Chanler inheritance be justified." [1]

Inspired by the example of a favorite great aunt, the activist and reformer Julia Ward Howe, Margaret Chanler Aldrich extended her spirit of service to the national level as a leader in the sufferage and prohibition movements. Her valiant and resourceful work as a Red Cross volunteer nurse in the Spanish-American War earned her a Congressionl Medal and helped bring about the creation of the first army nursing corps in American military history. [2]

Like her grandfather, sister, brother, and brother-in-law, Margaret Chanler Aldrich was also a poet. Although she produced two volumes of published poetry in her lifetime, she considered herself what she called a "poet in private." In her poetry, she reveals the private emotional power underlying the flinty public persona and deeply held principles for which she is commonly known.

In an Old Graveyard

Margaret Chanler Aldrich

The youngest Burthen in this field
Has known a century of sleep;
To this small pasturage of God
There comes no stricken files to weep.

The little children who look down
From scattered farms among the hills
Rest elsewhere, when they too are old
And leave the sum of human ills.

No name, no date, at head or foot,
Carve but this legend on my stone:
"He knew the world and chose to lie
Where earth and heaven are all alone."

The "sweet virgilia tree" in the following poem, published in 1914, still blossoms today at Rokeby.

In My Garden

Margaret Chanler Aldrich

Beneath the sweet virgilia tree
    I watched a saint arise.
What time the boughs were veiled in bloom
    That seemed from Paradise.

The saint laid blossoms to her cheek,
    God knows which shone most white, -
And cried, "O little tree, I dreamt
    About you yesternight.

"I dreamt the Lord God spoke in Heaven
    Saying, 'My child, a tree
Doth shroud to-night the song of souls
    Which know felicity.'

"These grape-like flowers in my dream
    Were beckoning to me;
While from an inner fragrance sang
    A golden-bodied bee."

Then swaying clusters hid the saint
    Deeper beneath their screen.
The petals dropped where stood her feet
    Made snow of summer's green.

And low I heard her voice of faith,
    "Sting, little bee! thy part
It is to teach the song of souls
    Sting close above my heart."

In February of 1916, Margaret Chanler Aldrich's nephew Victor Chapman became one of the most fearless members of the French Foreign Legion's "Escadrille Lafayette" - a squadron of American flyers fighting for France in WWI. Chapman was shot down over German enemy lines in June of 1916. His body was never found.

Victor Emmanuel Chapman

Margaret Chanler Aldrich

On quiet roads I see you most
Where elm shoots branch and sumachs glow;
Each tangle in the high hedge row
Clasps some strong greeting from your ghost.

On quiet roads all undisturbed
With woodchucks and with weeds you grew.
The humble things your spirit knew
Met stars and winter unperturbed.

On quiet roads no other came
Around rough sudden turns at dawn,
Riding with gestures of a fawn
The fleet-foot colt you would not tame.

The quiet roads received your soul
A tiny puzzle-headed boy
Whose pony was his only toy,
The long way home his only goal.

The quiet roads released your soul,
Ready to harness cloud with wind,
The chart in highest air to find
And from a fragment guide the whole.

The quiet roads scarce know this earth,
Her life, her graves, to them are one;
They look to see you in the sun
Or when new stars are brought to birth.

(August, 1916 - Rokeby)

(In 1918, Aldrich harnessed poetry's emotional power to defend a controversial new policy that would have allowed the War Department to severely limit the sharing of information on WWI American casualties. The poem was published in The New York Times *on March 24, 1918.)*

The Soldier to His Mother

Margaret Chanler Aldrich

If I am killed, let not my death betray
The regiment: Better a thousand times
That without lowered flags and holy chimes
You pass unknowing through my funeral day.
Fallen with honor, must I lead the way
For all who seek to find our guarded lines?
My name and way of going, are they signs
You make the enemy? Mother, I pray,
In mourning me, kill not some valiant mate.
Let silence be my shroud, with each advance
I fight to save you from the awful fate
Of Belgian mothers; if I die, the date
And place are all a matter of grim chance.
Till Victory! Your Son, Somewhere in France!

Fireflies

Margaret Chanler Aldrich

Crossing the fields with fireflies
Now bright now dark before my eyes,
I see a thing of clumsy sense
Beside their darting competence.
Skimming a hundred mimic seas,
Shooting in golden galaxies,
Impinging on the firmament
A pulsing gleam from their content,
I know the Genius of Surprize
Is passing through those fireflies.

(July, 1938 - Rokeby)

(unpublished poem courtesy of J. Winthrop Aldrich)

Facing

Margaret Chanler Aldrich

I stood to see my face in a dream
Whose mirror was kind to me.
Gone were every line and seam
Which mark maturity.

I woke to wonder why splendid years
With all the spirit knows,
As a worn and rigid map appears,
And into parchment grows.

(March, 1951)

(unpublished poem courtesy of J. Winthrop Aldrich)

Illustration: Miss Margaret Livingston Chanler
Town and Country *Magazine (1903)*
(New York Public Library)
(from a portrait by William Sergeant Kendall,
Rokeby Collection)

Three Wise Men

Margaret Chanler Aldrich

As I was homeward walking
　Across a world in tune,
I heard two wise men talking
　"What is there new in June?"

"What is there new in June?" I cried,
　And here a cuckoo fluttered,
"Where are your eyes, O great and wise,
　What nonsense have you uttered?"

One said, "We hoped great things from Brown,
　He is so persevering,
But what is new proves rarely true,
　Impatience interfering."

I plunged my hands into the earth,
　And drew out budding lilies,
I threw them sweet, before the feet
　Of those astonished sillies.

One gave the Latin name, and said
　"A false hybridization,
Geranium shoot can take club root
　In single segregation."

Again I heard the cuckoo mock,
　And he who was the greater
Said, "In July we're printing my
　New slant of the Equator."

As I was slowly walking
　Across the world in June,
I learned that to be talking
　Is not to be in tune.

I did not write these verses then,
　But in a drear December,
When even those two Spring-blind men
　Are pleasant to remember.

Joel E. Spingarn *(1875-1939)*

The Amenia estate of Troutbeck, once so beloved by poets Joel and Myron Benton and their friend John Burroughs, passed to a new generation of poet-scholars when it was purchased by Professor Joel E. Spingarn in 1910.

In that same year, the young Columbia University Professor of Comparative Literature coined the now familiar phrase "New Criticism" in his provocative call for a new form of literary analysis based solely on textual evidence.

A year later, Spingarn left Academia forever, ending his twelve year career at Columbia after being dismissed for defending a colleague embroiled in a romantic scandal. He considered this a fortunate escape from a disheartening professorial life with little, if any, real academic freedom (on the 25th anniversary of his dismissal, Spingarn held a party to celebrate his escape from an academic fate).

After serving as an army officer in WWI, he devoted himself to the cause of civil rights. Spingarn became a prominent leader in the NAACP for 26 years until his death in 1939, serving twice as NAACP president.

As a founder in 1919 of the publishing firm Harcourt, Brace and Company, Spingarn used his position as senior editor to encourage the publication of works by African American authors. Publishing proved a useful way for Spingarn to continue shaping American intellectual life outside the constraints of the university system he deplored.

At Troutbeck, he hosted two landmark civil rights conferences (known as the "Amenia Conferences") in 1916 and 1933, in additon to lecturing across America on the need for a "new abolitionism" that would emancipate African Americans from segregation, disenfranchisement and bigotry. In 1940, Spingarn's dear friend, W.E.B. DuBois dedicated his autobiography to Spingarn with the words, "To keep the memory of Joel Spingarn - Scholar and Knight."

Spingarn added much to Troutbeck's legendary beauty in his singularly intense devotion to the clematis vine. He first became enamored with clematis on a visit to England in 1927. But when he attempted to purchase plants upon his return, he found the species vitually unknown among American nurserymen. He eventually became a leading international expert on the clematis plant and stocked Troutbeck with an amazing collection of over 250 clematis varieties.

In 1936, *The New Yorker* magazine observed that "...when he [Spingarn] has nothing better to do, he drops into florist shops and asks what they have in the way of clematis. Nine times out of ten the florists are puzzled and finally say, 'Oh, you mean clematis.' Mr. Spingarn then recites to them a tart little poem he has written about the pronunciation of the word:

> Because it climbs a lattice,
> Hoi polloi say 'clem-at'-is;"
> But Webster's will not cease to hiss
> Until they call it 'clem'-a-tis.'" [1]

When the original Benton home at Troutbeck burned in 1916, Spingarn and his wife Amy built the manor house we know today as the Troutbeck Inn and Conference Center. The Spingarn's lovely estate was often visited by many of the leading writers, activists and political reformers of the 1920s and 30s.

The Poet

Joel E. Spingarn

I have not gathered these dreams out of the read-
    ing of books;
  They came to me, flowers of dusk, sweet with
      the odors of stars;
Some of them live not a day out of their shadowy
    nooks;
  Some of them still show the touch where my
      fingers bruised them with scars.

Spring Passion

Joel E. Spingarn

Blue sky, green fields, and lazy yellow sun.
  Why should I hunger for the burning South,
Where beauty needs no travail to be won,
  Now I may kiss her pure impassioned mouth?

Winds ripening with the rich delight of spring!
  Why should I yearn for myriad-colored skies,
Lit by auroral suns, when I may sing
  The flame and rapture of her starry eyes?

Oh, the songs of birds, and flowers fair to see!
  Why should I thirst for far off Eden-isles,
When I may hear her discourse melody,
  And bask, a dreamer, in her dreamy smiles?

Love's Wisdom

Joel E. Spingarn

Was I not born for other things than this:
  To dream within the shadows of my room,
  To waste my youthful heart in studious gloom,
And in the weary past the present miss?
Was I not born to taste of deeper bliss
  Than blinding eyes in poring over books,
  When I had rather feed on woman's looks
And sob my soul out in a single kiss?

No, mine astronomy, your deep-set eyes,
  And your rich voice, my Latin and my Greek,
  And your dear love, my sole philosophy,
Scholar and sage might revolutionize:
    In you all language, learning, wisdom be,
  And all the ancients listen when you speak.

The magnificent vistas of College Hill have always inspired equally magnificent dreams. In 1836, Poughkeepsie's first developers selected this spot to build a grandiose replica of the Parthenon. The following generation of developers dreamed of turning the gloriously situated "parthenon" into a glamorous resort hotel; and in the late 19th century, millionaire John Guy Vassar envisioned College Hill as the site of a new county orphanage.

No dream for College Hill, however, has proven more powerful than that of bestowing it upon the people. Since 1892, when cough drop manufacturer William W. Smith donated funds for its purchase, College Hill has been a public park.

Although once famed for its band concerts, fireworks, Edwardian greenhouses, quaint Depression era picnic shelter, and nationally important rock garden, the modern era College Hill Park continues to struggle against the forces of urban decay.

In the following poem however, we are reminded that College Hill has always existed as more than just a park and will continue to inspire dreams.

Photo: College Hill Conservatory

To a Hill

E. Lucien Waithe
28 Cottage Street, Poughkeepsie

O Hill, supreme above the bordering plain,
Despise thou not my faltering footsteps here;
To thee for calm relief I come again,
Seeking thy balm of breeze so sweet and dear.
What wealth of feeling surges through my heart!
When on thy crest I stand and see afar,
The gorgeous bank of clouds, the unstained sky,
The ever-sailing lights of day that bar,
 With shot-resistant beams, the peering eye,
The running green, the gables far away.
Oh Hill, full many a century thou hast seen
The lordly boughs through speeding breezes sway,
And on thy breast the trunk firm rooted lean,
And many human loves that grew and died
Among thy restful foliage and flowers.
The setting sun each day thou has espied
Lighting the ambered west, flooding the bowers
With unmatched gold, and lifting many a heart
To realms of love's sweet balmy paradise.
And to the throne of God the sacred part
Of all the spheres, where all is blessed thrice,
Full-banishing all earthly cares, all vice,
O Hill thy spirit lured my soul to dream,
Recalling thoughts that drift on Lethe's stream.

(*Poughkeepsie Sunday Courier*
December 19, 1920)

Kimlin Cider Mill

Now protected for future generations following an eight year preservation battle, the Kimlin Cider Mill has long held a special place in Dutchess County history. From the time the Irish immigrant Kimlins first arrived in Dutchess County in 1850 until the closing of their family business in 1990, three generations of Kimlins pressed cider here on Cedar Avenue in Poughkeepsie.[1]

But what made this mill unique was the Kimlins' penchant for all things strange and curious. Their collection, once estimated at over 100,000 items, filled the Kimlin Cider Mill to the rafters with an astonishing (some said bewildering) array of objects. Fashioned into a self-styled "museum," the Kimlin collection was often the convenient final resting place for objects deaccessioned by Vassar Brothers Institute and various departments of nearby Vassar College.[2]

Not surprisingly, the mill became an attraction for local school groups who toured it every year - sipping cider and wandering among collections of fossils, agricultural implements, taxidermy, sleigh bells, Indian relics, medieval armor, china, silver, minerals, buttons, swords, guns, daggers, books, engravings, and even a coral and shell collection said to have belonged to Matthew Vassar as well as over 100 pieces of "souvenir" stone chipped from "famous ruins" of the world.

Visiting the Kimlin Mill was a particularly special part of the Vassar College experience. In his recollections of college life, college president Henry Noble MacCracken describes how each Vassar freshman class was introduced to the mill:

> ...something over two miles from the college gate, an old road ran south to the cider mill. Juniors always took their little sisters, the freshmen, for doughnuts and a glass of cider to the Kimlin's mill. They sat by hundreds along the old stone wall, singing college songs, and drinking the heart's blood of good Dutchess County apples. Then home again in gay groups, in the soft autumn glow, under the scarlet and gold of the maples.

President MacCracken and his wife frequently hiked to the mill and became good friends with the Kimlins. When Ralph Kimlin decided to start a guest book for the mill, he asked President MacCracken to make the first official entry. MacCracken cheerfully obliged with the following poem.

(In the opening lines, former English Professor MacCracken quotes from one of Chaucer's Canterbury Tales and sets up a joking comparison between Chaucer's Symkyn, a miller who lives in the village of Trumpington near the bawdy students of Cambridge's Soler Hall College and Kimlin, the cider maker who lives in the town of Poughkeepsie near the bit less bawdy women of Vassar College.)

> *"At Trumpyngton, not ferre fro Cantebrigge,*
> *Ther goth a brook, and over that a brigge,*
> *Upon whiche brigge there stant a melle,*
> *And this is verray sothe that I telle."*
> Still goes the brook, and still the Kasperkill
> Winds its slow way below the cider mill
> Where Vassar girls, perched on the wayside wall,
> Make merry like clerks of Soler Hall,
> With doughnuts, hot dogs, cider and with fun
> Less rowdy than the Scots at Trumpington.
> But Vassar "bumps" old Cambridge, 'tis confessed;
> Kimlin's pure cider's of the very best
> And though we make no special brag of morum,
> We're just a mite more careful of decorum.

临湖亭
轻舸迎上客
悠悠湖上来
当轩对樽酒
四面芙蓉开

Innisfree

The Millbrook estate of Innisfree, named for the magical setting of W.B. Yeats' celebrated poem, was the creation of painter Walter Beck and his wife, iron heiress Marion Stone Beck. Soon after their marriage in 1930, the couple moved to Mrs. Beck's 950 acre estate in Millbrook and set about building a charming recreation of "Wisley," a British Queen Anne manor house in Surrey.

But as the house approached completion and construction of the classic English gardens began, Walter Beck decided that Innisfree required a fresh source of inspiration for its grounds. Work on the gardens in Millbrook was suspended while the Becks conducted an intensive study of 8th century Chinese garden designer and poet Wang Wei whose work entranced them.

Wang Wei's design style, with its series of wondrous garden episodes unfolding along a seemingly aimless path, became Beck's inspiration for Innisfree's garden design. With a canvas consisting of the 20 acre Tyrrel Lake, three granite cliffs and the gently rolling hills of Dutchess County, the Becks - along with their landscape architect Lester Collins and a staff of 20 gardeners - began what turned out to be a magnificent experiment in oriental garden design.

After the Beck's died in the 1950s, the estate was opened to the public in 1960. The manor house was demolished in 1982 to enable better care and funding for the Innisfree gardens. Visitors today continue to seek out the magical qualities of this Dutchess County landscape forever linked to Yeats' poem, "The Lake Isle of Innisfree."

(Above)Translation from Chinese:
"At the Lake Pavillion" by Wang Wei
On a skiff I meet an honored guest,
Slowly, slowly, it comes across the lake.
Facing at the railing, we drink a cup of wine,
On all sides, lotus flowers are in bloom.

The Lake Isle of Innisfree

William Butler Yeats

I will arise and go now, and go to Innisfree,
And a small cabin build there, of clay and wattles made:
Nine bean-rows will I have there, a hive for the honey-bee;
And live alone in the bee-loud glade.

And I shall have some peace there, for peace comes dropping slow,
Dropping from the veils of the morning to where the cricket sings;
There midnight's all a glimmer, and noon a purple glow,
And evening full of the linnet's wings.

I will arise and go now, for always night and day
I hear lake water lapping with low sounds by the shore;
While I stand on the roadway, or on the pavements grey,
I hear it in the deep heart's core.

Locust Grove

When Miss Annette Innis Young died in 1975, she had lived on her family's Poughkeepsie estate of Locust Grove for 80 of her 90 years. Although the estate was already famous as the 19th century residence of artist and inventor Samuel Morse, it was Miss Young's generosity that ensured the remarkable preservation and public enjoyment of this Hudson Valley treasure, with its art collections and gardens intact in the heart of commercial and residential development.

Often we visit a "Great Estate" for its fascinating celebrity associations and splendid artistic finery. But on lucky occasions, we also catch a glimpse of the great estate as the real home of real people who even have pets. In the following circa 1940 poem by Annette Young's mother, Martha, we unexpectedly meet several generations of Locust Grove dogs who very clearly were once a cherished part of estate life. (In her will, Annette Young left $10,000 for the care of her 8 cats and 5 dogs - all of them strays.)

(poem and photos courtesy of Locust Grove Historic Site)

Photo: Annette Young (circa 1940)

Pet Cemetery

Martha Innis Young

Back from the drive - but not too far
Safe 'neath some trees where naught can mar
This hidden spot, then sleep at rest
The many dogs we loved best.

No ordered line of little stones
Mark out the ranks where lie the bones
Of those dear pals of yours and mine,
Those truest friends, tried, staunch, and fine.

The largest slab stone in this dear place
Has, as inscription, on its face
"Here lies old Rover, hence our tears,
The children's friend for many years."

A smaller tablet marks this spot
A Coach dog sleek, who was called "Dot"
His life was gay but all too short,
And next to him sleeps the shepherd "Sport."

Some lovely ferns guard and bend o'er
The little mound, which was of yore
The sweetest puppy of them all
A bunch of love, a wooley ball
Of fur and fun - a pest, a joy -
That little frisking "Tinker Boy."

The Major Domo, grand and grave
Was Dan the Dane, big, strong and brave
He's buried 'neath a sturdy oak
He knew so much he all but spoke.

A chiseled slab of grayish stone
Has carven at the top - a bone,
And Rajah's line to mark his might
Is tersely put, "He sure could fight."

Here's marker smart with gay rosette,
A Poodle's, french, was Annette's pet,
He was so vain and to a hair
His pon-pons must be trimmed with care.

There's many a more safe guarded grave
Whereon wild rose and daisies wave
And birds and squirrels send their Hails
To former friendly (?) wagging tails.

The place is rough, because we know,
The grass is long allowed to grow,
The way they liked to romp through it,
Play "hide and seek" and "miss and hit."

Flowers and ferns and shrubs and trees,
Guard well these little silent mounds,
And may my Heaven, be, at last,
The far off "Happy Hunting Grounds."

Frank S. Dickerson (1915-2004)

Poet Frank S. Dickerson grew up on a Revolutionary War era farm now part of the Casperkill Country Club in Poughkeepsie. He graduated from Oakwood Friends School and Cornell University, served as a field artillery major in WWII, and went on to a career as a college administrator and development officer - finally retiring to his home on Cape Cod.

His poetry poignantly evokes the Hudson Valley landscape of the early 20th century when Dutchess County's unspoiled beauty was the unforgettable backdrop to the adventures of Dickerson's youth.

Today Frank Dickerson's childhood home is known as the "Fort Homestead," an 18th century colonial farmhouse that narrowly avoided demolition in 2004.

(poems and photo courtesy of the Fort Homestead Association)

God's Country

Frank S. Dickerson

I shall go to Dutchess County and see Casper Creek,
and a hut I will build there of logs and of sticks,
a pool will I have there, and I shall seek
the fish that live there, and a bourbon to drink.

And I shall dwell there, live all alone,
seeking quiet and solace for a life that's been long.
Yes, I dwell there as I write this poem,
and there I find peace from the throng.

I go now for I long to see
old orchards in moonlight, the Hudson River,
the Hudson River leading to the sea.
Dutchess County. I'll not leave her again.

There are Memories

Frank S. Dickerson

There are memories
        of olden Dutchess County
they that fill my thoughts at the end of day,
of the golden shafts of sunlight in the meadow
and shaking poplar leaves across the way.

Mornings woke to patchy fog across damp glades
the ribald calls of fellows making hay,
then moonbeams came to blossom in the evening
as my girl and I savored stars'display.

There were rapid trout streams burbling through the woodland
a little bridge where phoebes came to nest,
there were pools where boys could swim buck naked
then come out on sun-warmed rocks to rest.

A Baldwin apple orchard far on the highland
staghorn sumac filling in a corner there,
next to bittersweet and ivy covered stone walls
I could look across the Hudson far away.

O, those golden thoughts of Dutchess County
of Vassar and the Kimlin cider mill,
as I age I have good fortune to remember
the nostalgic golden memories of Kaspar Kill.

For there are mem'ries of olden Dutchess County
they that fill my thoughts at the end of day,
of the golden shafts of sunlight in the meadow
and shaking poplar leaves across the way.

Choose a firm cloud before it fall,
and in it
Catch, ere she change, the Cynthia
of this minute.

          -Alexander Pope

Cynthia

Frank S. Dickerson

We walked a rural lane together
then sat upon an autumn ridge
the silver moon above
and gazed across vapoured fields
the evening young.

Far off the Hudson flowed
gently toward the sea
though none on that ridge could see
the strength of water quietly
pushing southward brought us close
silently urging us intimately.

We touched hands and then retreated
 we bended speaking words
       of philosophy
then rose to walk softly
       toward the Hudson
our river leading to the sea.

Alas, I've not since
       seen Cynthia
she may have changed.
She was a moon girl.
It was September.

Fala

On a lovely April Sunday in 1945, FDR was laid to rest in Hyde Park. His Scottish Terrier Fala attended the ceremony in the care of FDR's dear friend Daisy Suckley of Wilderstein. In her diary, Suckley recorded that Fala "gave a sharp bark" after each volley of the West Point cadet rifles, in what she felt was "an unconscious salute of his own to his master..." [1]

Although Daisy Suckley had given Fala to FDR as a Christmas gift in 1940 and had cared for Fala frequently, the Roosevelt children asked that Fala be allowed to reside with Eleanor Roosevelt after their father's death. In 1958, Mrs. Roosevelt wrote in her newspaper column, "Fala accepted me after my husband's death, but I was just someone to put up with until the master should return. Many dogs eventually forget. I felt that Fala never really forgot." [2]

Fala is buried near FDR in the rose garden of the Hyde Park presidential library. Since 1997, this most famous of all presidential pets has been memorialized alongside FDR in a sculpture by Neil Estern at the FDR Memorial on the National Mall.

After FDR's death, images of the well known Fala bereft of his beloved master touched the grieving nation with a particular poignancy. Daisy Suckley received the following poem after FDR's death and kept it for 47 years until her death in 1991.

(poem courtesy of Wilderstein Historic Site)

Fala

He stood and gazed at the empty chair,
Wondering why his master was not there,
Why he received no gentle pat
When by the side of the chair he sat;
Ah, little Fala, with sad, sad eyes,
You have lost a master, kind and wise,
It is hard for you to understand,
Why you never again will feel his hand;
Little dog of the faithful heart,
In his life you played an important part;
To you he turned at the end of the day,
No matter how tired, for a bit of play,
You understood his every mood,
This gentle master, kind and good;
You know not why a gulf so wide
Has taken him forever, from your side;
But litle Fala, he'll understand,
And in that other far off land,
He'll be glad because the heart of you
In death, as in life, is ever true.

Written April 15, 1945
By J. Helen Caughey
Winnipeg, Canada

Franklin Delano Roosevelt

"Invictus" is widely considered among the best known and best loved of all Victorian poems. Its author, British poet and journalist William Ernest Henley (1849-1903) suffered from a form of tuberculosis which resulted in the amputation of his left leg and the near loss of his right leg. Despite the limited forms of treatment available to him and the poor chances for his recovery, Henley overcame his illness and his handicap as well.

FDR considered "Invictus"one of his favorite poems, and perhaps in the darkest hours of his life, he gathered strength from Henley's affirmation of heroic human dignity in the face of even the most overwhelming suffering and injustice.

Few poems have seized the public imagination the way "Invictus" once did. Henley's poetic evocation of the unconquerable human spirit was often memorized by British and American children who grew up in the era when committing poems to memory was a standard component of school curriculums.

And for some, the poem remains an unforgettable touchstone. Presidential speechwriter, Peggy Noonan recalls in her memoirs that while working for Ronald Reagan, she thought often of FDR since to her, he seemed "the modern President who had sounded most like a President." As she set about crafting the Reagan style, her thoughts also turned to "Invictus:"

...I had read about Roosevelt over the years and knew he liked the poem "Invictus" - 'I am the master of my fate/I am the captain of my soul' - and saw now that he had absorbed its rhythm so that it had become his own triumphant cadence, a sound that echoed not only in his speeches but even in his recorded conversation. I'd think: this is how Reagan should sound. [1]

More recently, Presidential candidate Senator John McCain baffled reporters by quoting a line from "Invictus." When he later revealed he had memorized the poem as a student, an editorial in the *New York Times* labelled him a "Neo-Victorian." [2]

Invictus

William Ernest Henley

Out of the night that covers me,
  Black as the Pit from pole to pole,
I thank whatever gods may be
  For my unconquerable soul.

In the fell clutch of Circumstance
  I have not winced nor cried aloud.
Under the bludgeonings of Chance
  My head is bloody, but unbowed.

Beyond this place of wrath and tears
  Looms but the Horror of the shade,
And yet the menace of the years
  Finds, and shall find, me unafraid.

It matters not how strait the gate,
  How charged with punishments the scroll,
I am the master of my fate:
  I am the captain of my soul.

Eleanor Roosevelt

When 21 year old Harvard Junior Franklin Roosevelt proposed to his 19 year old fifth cousin Eleanor in 1903, she accepted - but not without taking the rather unusual first step of evaluating his reaction to the 1846 poem "A Woman's Shortcomings" by Elizabeth Barrett Browning.

At age 19, Eleanor had uneasily assumed the role of society debutante. Doubtless, she observed many young women like the one in Browning's poem even though her plain looks and somber manner kept her somewhat detached from the social whirl. She later admitted, "I knew I was the first girl in my mother's family who was not a belle and, though I never acknowledged it to them at that time, I was deeply ashamed." [1]

Eleanor's definition of love as expressed in Browning's poem, was certainly not that of a shallow "belle," and to her joy, Franklin reassured her that he truly did love her in that way. Her niece wrote later, "The way that my Aunt Eleanor felt about Franklin was the way she had felt about her father. It was the fantastic love that she felt would be total." [2]

In her autobiography, Eleanor reveals that when she told her grandmother about her engagement, her grandmother had asked if she was really in love: "I solemnly answered 'yes,' and yet I know now that it was years before I understood what being in love or loving really meant." [3]

A Woman's Shortcomings

Elizabeth Barrett Browning

She has laughed as softly as if she sighed,
She has counted six, and over,
Of a purse well filled, and a heart well tried -
Oh, each a worthy lover!
They "give her time," for her soul must slip
Where the world has set the grooving;
She will lie to none with her fair red lip:
But love seeks truer loving.

She trembles her fan in a sweetness dumb,
As her thoughts were beyond recalling;
With a glance for one, and a glance for some,
From her eyelids rising and falling;
Speaks common words with a blushful air,
Hears bold words, unreproving;
But her silence says - what she never will swear -
And love seeks better loving.

Go, lady! lean to the night-guitar,
And drop a smile to the bringer,
Then smile as sweetly, when he is far,
At the voice of an in-door singer.
Bask tenderly beneath tender eyes;
Glance lightly, on their removing;
And join new vow to old perjuries -
But dare not call it loving!

Unless you can think, when the song is done,
No other is soft in the rhythm;
Unless you can feel, when left by One,
That all men else go with him;
Unless you can know when unpraised by his breath,
That your beauty itself wants proving;
Unless you can swear "For life, For death!" -
Oh, fear to call it loving!

Unless you can muse in a crowd all day
On the absent face that fixed you;
Unless you can love as the angels may,
With the breath of heaven betwixt you;
Unless you can dream that his faith is fast,
Through behoving and unbehoving;
Unless you can die when the dream is past -
Oh, never call it loving!

Chanler Chapman
(1901-1982)

Chanler Armstrong Chapman was the son of two brilliant parents, social critic and poet John Jay Chapman and the eldest Astor orphan Elizabeth Chanler.

Chapman spent much of his life in Barrytown on the family estate of Sylvania, mostly living in an estate cottage called "Good Hap" while operating a marginal dairy farm. From 1958 to 1982, he also published an idiosyncratic monthly newspaper called the *Barrytown Explorer*, cofounded with his second wife Helen.

Chapman was a well known Dutchess County character who lived life with an eccentric, blustering fervor that once encountered, few ever forgot. A self-proclaimed "bad boy" at prep school and an undergraduate bootlegger at Harvard, Chapman found his short-lived career in journalism a bore. Horse racing, women and plotting against the Nazis were far more entertaining. He was a brusque and sometimes surprising poet who wrote sonnets in his bathrobe before breakfast and marched around town in his signature bib overalls.

Chapman married three times, noting he had inherited his mother's "inconvenient but interesting" tendency to take chances on love. In all his relationships, there was a mixture of volatility and erudition that was as daunting as it was fascinating. A young Bard student who became a writer for the *Barrytown Explorer* later remembered, "In all honesty, I must admit I always approached the door at Good Hap with a certain trepidation. After all it was difficult to predict what would occur on the other side...Chanler proved completely unable to remember my name unless prompted, and not always then. I still treasure the evening he introduced me to his other dinner guests as George Washington Smith." [1]

In memoirs he unfortunately did not live to complete, Chapman reflected darkly on his family legacy and the celebrated "river estates" that shaped him:

Sylvania and Rokeby, adjoining country places, are laced into my memory like two vivid snakes which tangle me in their coils. The tangles of early environment are strong. If you stay around they will engulf you, swallow you whole after they have crushed every bone in your body and strangled you. The pleasure dome of the parent becomes the deadly arena of the second generation, a place of blood and sand where the exits are used by live beasts and dead gladiators who have been eaten up by their possessions. [2]

Chapman's poetry appeared regularly in the *Barrytown Explorer* in his favorite form, the 14 line sonnet. His monthly compilation of one or two sentence observations on Hudson Valley life also occasionally bordered on the poetic - much like the 19th century local news column of Poughkeepsie journalist George W. Davids.

April 27, 1959 (from *The Barrytown Explorer*)

(local news column by Chanler Chapman)

Eat your shad roe now.
It's never the same frozen.
Fresh roe is a rare delicacy.
The sooner it's cooked the finer it tastes.
Out of the river and into the pan makes the best roe.
Why say hard things about homogenized cigar wrappers?
Because they taste different.
Tobacco homogenized into paper tastes like paper.
Make mine the straight leaf.
Two months to fresh corn.
The cob should go straight from garden to pot.
Ever eat corn that travelled?
You can taste the weariness of the transportation.
The sunshine leaks out.
Gather horseradish now.
It's fresh and hot.
Later it's too hot.
Mint comes later. So do the juleps.
Running water, cow manure and lime. Under these conditions cress
will grow like hair on a dog.
The herring are running. So are the outboard motors Saturdays and
Sundays.
The river has its friends.
In the mouth of the Mudderkill Creek three men last Sunday picked up
a 3-ft. pickerel in their hands.

Diurnal Message

Go down, red sun, behind the blue Catskills,
Easeful and cool, slowly fades the day.
Drop to the west. The River works its way
On a mile-wide rising tide. The Valley fills
With shadow. As the sun hangs on the hills
Before its final wink it seems to say:
"Perhaps I am the last for you. This may
Be your quietus, the last flash that kills."
This could be true, but I prefer to think
The setting sun, flashing its final wink
Suggests eternity of endless time.
Another evening darkens into night,
Prepares the pause to catch another light -
Another dawn to write another rhyme.

- C.A.C.

September, 1967

Let What May Transpire

Ah yes, my dear, your well-known woman's charm,
Vivacity and wit, - the flash of gold
That floods like gathering dawn, fold after fold,
Your startling laugh that strikes but does no harm, -
Remember these when age brings in a calm
As deep as sleep. Then stir yourself. Be bold
To recollect this feeling when you're old.
Forever is forever - arm in arm.

Make headway as you can. Time calls the tune.
Your laughter is immortal while it lasts.
When old age warms herself before a fire
Of cooling ashes, - let what may transpire.
Though Winter howls outside with angry blasts
You'll know you once were lovely as the moon.

- C.A.C.

December, 1972

Mock the Guy

You know, at least you ought to know, that I
Feel better since you've been around. I think
The bread and butter - merest food and drink-
Taste better now. There's magic in the sky.
Dull chores that once would make me almost cry
Now skip along. You are the missing link -
My ball and chain - and you will surely wink
At me contemptuously before I die.

Look up, my Ida. Growl your usual greeting.
Turn on the light at night and look at me.
Saint Patrick's Day is here. Spring is repeating
The nonsense of the buds and birds for us.
Snowdrops and Irish Whiskey and black tea
Blend in the end - make death ridiculous.

              - C.A.C.
                     March, 1973

The Barrytown Explorer
(1958-1982)

The eclectic monthly newspaper published by Chanler Chapman from 1958 until his death in 1982 explored a wide variety of topics - from politics and local history to biography, music, gossip, and poetry. In some ways, Chapman was actually creating a 20th century version of an old-fashioned 19th century local paper - where even poetry (on any topic and in varying degrees of proficiency) enjoyed a refreshing return to prominence.

The following four poems demonstrate the range of local interest poetry printed in the *Barrytown Explorer*.

No Bones About It

Shad is the Hudson's noblest fish
But gracious, isn't it bony!
Serving up such a gritty dish
Can tarnish matrimony.
But here's a way to get your wish
For shad smooth as macaroni:
Wipe, then butter; of lemon, a swish;
Foil-wrap without parsimony.
Bake at two-hundred-fifty-ish,
SIX HOURS, for here time is money.
Unwrap and season. It tastes delish -
With nary a spine or wee bony.

H.R.C.
(*Barrytown Explorer* April 27, 1959)

(written by Chanler Chapman's wife Helen, a frequent Barrytown Explorer *columnist and contributor of poetry until her death in 1970)*

Hudson River Bracketed

Paris Leary

Bryant's silent redskin with his harvest warpaint
treads like a tachiste past the Minor Seminary
where the holy boys in brown skirts are playing soccer,
to meld with an instant copse where the crunch road
hangs over the Hudson. In our part of the valley
there are fields of apples thick with trucks and pickers,
crumbled miles of dry-stone spiked with goldenrod,
sumacs on their way, and paved drives leading,
they say, to the invisible houses of the vieux riches.

Our Dutchers sailed rivers like seas, bringing cheese, gin,
and John Calvin, leaving their names and Reformed Churches
to tourists and the Irish: - Rhinecliff, Fishkill, Staatsburg,
Germantown...over in Tivoli now they marry
their cousins and kids stop on the street to stare
if you slow your car to look in at Staibs Bar and Grill;
and in Rhinebeck at the Beekman Arms Republican ladies
with blue hair and muscular legs click their teeth
on pineapple hamsteak and deplore the times.

There is a high ground-mist with twilight under it
along the River Road. In our part of the valley
it is a long evening and the black fruit of crows
ripens, motionless, on the white birches. It is time
for the old women and small children to come from the grey
houses trimmed with white and walk to Evensong
along the River Road past the cider-mill.
But over the valley, over our part of the valley,
in the winds which move the pines along the River Road
there is an air of ineluctable regret
because the young Episcopal priest is a go-getter from Cleveland.

(*Barrytown Explorer*, September 1962)

The Hitchhiker

Lorraine Freeman

Christ tried to hitch hike into Tivoli today
He got as far as 9G
but no one would pick him up

the first car was full of migrant workers
who thought He was a farmer
the second car was full of farmers
who thought He was a migrant worker
the third car was full of Bard students
who thought He was the fuzz
the fourth car was full of the fuzz
who thought He was a Bard student
the fifth car was full of Republicans
who thought He was a Democrat
the sixth car was full of Democrats
who thought He was a Republican
the seventh car was full of Negroes
who thought He was white
the eighth car was full of whites
who thought he was a Negro
the ninth car was full of men
who though He was an animal
the last car was full of animals
who thought He was a MAN

Christ tried to hitch hike into Tivoli today
he got as far as 9G
but no one picked him up

(*Barrytown Explorer*, January 1970)

William Geckle was a poet, author and advertising executive for the Luckey Platt Department Store in Poughkeepsie. When his wife insisted that his poetry would make wonderful song lyrics, Geckle decided to contact "the only singer and song writer we knew, Pete Seeger." Five of Geckle's poems were put to music and recorded by Seeger in 1976 on the album "Fifty Sail on Newburgh Bay." "The Moon in the Pear Tree" is based on a memory aid once used by sloop skippers to remember the moon's effect on the river's tide. (The moon in apogee was remembered as "the moon in the apple tree" while the moon in perigee was remembered as "the moon in the pear tree.")

The Moon in the Pear Tree

William Geckle

Look up, sailor, and you'll see,
The moon hangin' up in the old pear tree,
The old pear tree on the crest of the hill,
While the moon draws the tide and the rivers fill.
What better can a sailor hope to see
Than the moon hangin' up in the old pear tree!

Look up, sailor, and you'll see
The moon hangin' up in the apple tree,
The apple tree grows in the yard out back
And the moon holds the tide and the water back.
So a sailor's never very glad to see
The moon hangin' up in the apple tree.

Look up, sailor, and don't be sad,
The moon and the tide are bringin' up shad,
The shad and salmon and the sturgeon too,
 Comin' up the River like they used to do.
 So look up, sailor, and hope to see
The moon hangin' up in the old pear tree.

Look ahead, sailor, and you'll see,
Times a-comin' back like they used to be,
When the water's clear and way up high
Once more you see stars in a clear blue sky.
What better can a sailor hope to see
Than times comin' back like they used to be!

(*Barrytown Explorer*, November 1978)

Notes

Henry A. Livingston
1. Don Foster, *Author Unknown* (New York: Henry Holt and Company, 2000), 247.
2. James Thurber, "A Visit from St. Nicholas in the Ernest Hemingway Manner," *The New Yorker* (December 24, 1927).
3. Henry Noble MacCracken, *Blithe Dutchess* (New York: Hastings House, 1958) 370-390.

William Wilson
1. William Wilson and Benson J. Lossing (ed.), *Poems* (Poughkeepsie: A. Wilson, 1881) 3.

Maria James
1. Rufus Wilmot Griswold, *The Female Poets of America* (New York: Parry and McMillan, 1854) 66.
2. Ibid., 67.
3. Maria James, *Wales and Other Poems* (New York: John S. Taylor, 1839) 22.

Fitz-Greene Halleck
1. John W.M. Hallock, *The American Byron: Homosexuality and the Fall of Fitz-Greene Halleck* (University of Wisconsin Press, 2000).
2. Joel Benton, "Reminiscences of Eminent Lecturers," *Harper's Magazine* (March, 1898).
3. James Grant Wilson, *The Life and Letters of Fitz-Greene Halleck* (New York: D. Appleton and Company, 1869), 482.
4. Ibid., 477.
5. Marvin Olasky, "Fleeting Fame," *World Magazine* (July 28, 2007).

Rokeby
1. "La Bergerie/Rokeby" *Historic American Buildings Survey* (NY - No. 5623), 12; Oral History: J. Winthrop Aldrich, Rokeby.

Springside
1. Benson Lossing, *Vassar College and Its Founder* (New York: C.A. Alvord, 1867), 60.

Founder's Day
1. Elizabeth Hazelton, *The Autobiography and Letters of Matthew Vassar* (New York: Oxford University Press, 1916), 195.

Myron Benton
1. John Burroughs, "Myron Benton," *The Magazine of Poetry* Volume II (Buffalo: Charles Wells Moulton, 1890), 277.

2. Edward J. Renehan, Jr., *John Burroughs: An American Naturalist* (Hensonville, NY: Black Dome Press, 1992), 62.
3. Burroughs, *The Magazine of Poetry*, 277.

Joel Benton
1. Joel Benton, "Reminiscences of Eminent Lecturers," *Harper's Magazine* (March, 1898) 603.
2. Ibid., 610.
3. Joel Benton, *Persons and Places* (New York: Broadway Publishing Company) 2-5.

Edward Hazen Parker
1. Edward Hazen Parker, *Life's Race Well Run with a Sketch of Its History* (Poughkeepsie: Hiram S. Wiltsie, 1884), 11.
2. "Notes," *The Magazine of Poetry* (Charles Wells Moulton, 1892), 240.
3. Parker, *Life's Race.*
4. Henry Noble MacCracken, *Blithe Dutchess* (New York: Hastings House, 1958) 410.

Wallace Bruce
1. Wallace Bruce, *From the Hudson to the Yosemite* (New York: American News Company, 1884), End notes.
2. "Reception to Mr. Bruce," *Poughkeepsie Daily Eagle* (October 28, 1893).

William Harloe
1."Obituary" *Poughkeepsie Daily Eagle* (February 2, 1891).

Josh Billings
1. *Poughkeepsie News-Press* (May, 26, 1884).
2. *Poughkeepsie News-Press* (July 9, 1885), Francis Shubael Smith, *Life and Adventures of Josh Billings* (New York: G.W. Carleton, 1883), 45.
3. John Clark Ridpath, "Josh Billings," *The Ridpath Library of Universal Literature* (Philadelphia: Avil Printing Company, 1903), 444.
4. Josh Billings and Thomas Nast, *The Complete Works of Josh Billings (pseud.)* (New York: G.W. Dillingham, 1876) 489.

George W. Davids
1. "George W. Davids is Dead," *Poughkeepsie Daily Eagle* (February 1, 1894).
2. Ibid.
3. Ibid.

Vassar College
1. Henry Noble MacCracken, *The Hickory Limb* (New York: Charles Scribner's Sons, 1950), 81.

Maria Mitchell

1. Phebe Mitchell Kendall, *Maria Mitchell: Life, Letters and Journals* (Boston: Lee and Shepard, 1896), 178.
2. Ibid., 186.
3. Ibid., 177.
4. "Maria Mitchell at Vassar," *Poughkeepsie Daily Eagle* (November 8, 1889).

Edna St. Vincent Millay

1. Nancy Milford, *Savage Beauty: The Life of Edna St.Vincent Millay* (New York: Random House, 2001), 93.
2. Edna St. Vincent Millay and Holly Peppe (ed.), *Early Poems of Edna St. Vincent Millay* (New York: Penguin Group, 1998), XIII.
3. Milford, *Savage Beauty*, 110.
4. Ibid., 114.
5. Millay, Peppe, *Early Poems*, XIV.

Riverview Academy

1. Advertisment for Riverview Military Academy, June 1901.

Poughkeepsie Regatta

1. John W. and Stephen J. Lundin, "Cornell's Influence on Washington and West Coast Rowing," 2005 *(www.rowinghistory.net)*.
2. *Poughkeepsie Sunday Courier* (June 28, 1896).
3. Lundin, "Cornell's Influence."
4. "A Joyous Celebration," *Poughkeepsie Daily Eagle* (June 26, 1897).

Dutchess County Courthouse

1. *Poughkeepsie News-Telegraph* (July 20, 1889).

John Jay Chapman

1. Lately Thomas, *The Astor Orphans: A Pride of Lions* (New York: W. Morrow, 1971), 141.
2. Edmund Wilson, *The Triple Thinkers* (New York: Harcourt, Brace and Company, 1938), 186.
3. Ibid., 168.

Margaret Chanler Aldrich

1. Lately Thomas, *The Astor Orphans: A Pride of Lions.* (New York: W. Morrow, 1971), 281.
2. Ibid., 141.

Joel E. Spingarn

1. Russell Maloney, "Accent on Clem," *The New Yorker* (March 21, 1936).

Kimlin Cider Mill

1. "Golden Nectar Made from Fruit of Famous Orchards," *Pough-*

keepsie Sunday Courier (December 1, 1935).
2. Helen Myers, "Volens and Valens," *Poughkeepsie New Yorker* (February 8, 1948).
3. Henry Noble MacCracken, *The Hickory Limb* (New York: Charles Scribner's Sons, 1950), 117.

Fala
1. Geoffrey C. Ward, *Closest Companion: The Unknown Story of the Intimate Friendship between Franklin Roosevelt and Margaret Suckley* (Boston: Houghton Mifflin Company, 1995), 422.
2. "FDR's Fala: World's Most Famous Dog," *(www.bushybarney.tripod.com)*.

Franklin Delano Roosevelt
1. Peggy Noonan, "Confessions of a White House Speechwriter," *New York Times Sunday Magazine* (October 15, 1989).
2. William Kristol, "Thoroughly Unmodern McCain," *New York Times* (January 21, 2008).

Eleanor Roosevelt
1. Eleanor Roosevelt, *The Autobiography of Eleanor Roosevelt* (DaCapo Press, 1992), 37.
2. Janice Pottker, *Sara and Eleanor* (New York: MacMillan, 2004), 193.
3. Roosevelt, *Autobiography*, 41.

Chanler Chapman
1. George A. Smith, "His Irrepressible Spirit, His Vital Enthusiasm" *The Barrytown Explorer* (April, 1982).
2. Chanler Chapman, "Memoirs, July 1970" *The Barrytown Explorer* (January, 1982).

Acknowledgments:

Special thanks to Annon Adams, Wint Aldrich, Ginny Buechele, Ellie Charwat, Nan Fogel, Eileen Hayden, Lynn Lucas, Steve Mann, Malcolm Mills, Dean Rogers, Willa Skinner, Ken Snodgrass, Greg Sokaris, and Lisa Weiss. Deepest gratitude to the poets of Dutchess County whose work leads us to discover both our history and our better selves.

Sources

Henry A. Livingston

Foster, Don. *Author Unknown*. New York: Henry Holt and Company, 2000.

MacCracken, Henry Noble. *Blithe Dutchess*. New York: Hastings House, 1958.

"Not Much of a Clatter." *New York Times* (December 22, 2007).

Poughkeepsie Journal (December 22, 1968) (November 27, 1977).

Reynolds, Helen Wilkinson. "The Story of Locust Grove." *Dutchess County Historical Society Year Book* 1932, 21-32.

Thurber, James. "A Visit from St. Nicholas in the Ernest Hemingway Manner." *The New Yorker* (December 24, 1927).

Van Deusen, Mary. Henry Livingston, Jr. website (www.iment.com).

William Wilson

Leslie, Stephen and Sidney Lee, George Smith. "William Wilson," *Dictionary of National Biography*. Oxford University Press, 1900.

Ross, John Dawson. *Scottish Poets in America*. Pagan and Ross, 1889.

Wilson, James Grant. *The Poets and Poetry of Scotland*. Harper and Brothers, 1876.

Wilson, William and Benson Lossing (ed.). *Poems*. Poughkeepsie: A. Wilson, 1881.

Maria James

Griswold, Rufus Wilmot. *The Female Poets of America*. Parry and McMillan, 1854.

James, Maria. *Wales and Other Poems*. New York: John S. Taylor, 1839.

Fitz-Greene Halleck

Benton, Joel. "Some Once Famous Names" *Literary Collector: A*

Monthly Magazine of Booklore and Bibliography. G.D. Smith, 1903.

Cody, Michael. *Dictionary of Literary Biography*. Gale Group, 2004.

Cozzens, Frederic S. *Fitz-Greene Halleck: A Memorial*. New York: Trow and Smith, 1868.

Duyckinck, Everet and George. *Cyclopaedia of American Literature*. Charles Scribner, 1856.

"Fitz-Greene Halleck." *Putnam's Magazine*. G.P. Putnam and Son, 1868.

"Fitz-Greene Halleck." *The Eclectic Magazine*. New York: Leavitt, Trow and Company, 1868.

Halleck, Fitz-Greene and Joseph Rodman Drake. *The Croakers*. New York: Bradford Club, 1860.

Hallock, John W. M. *The American Byron: Homosexuality and the Fall of Fitz-Greene Halleck*. University of Wisconsin Press, 2000.

Haralson, Eric and John Hollander. *Encyclopedia of American Poetry: The 19th Century*. Chicago: Fitzroy Dearborn, 1998.

"Here Astor Once Lived." *New York Times* (February 16, 1896).

Griswold, Rufus Wilmot. *The Poets and Poetry of America*. Parry and McMillan, 1856.

Long, Augustus White. *American Poems 1776-1900*. New York: American Book Company, 1905.

Olasky, Marvin. "Fleeting Fame." *World Magazine* (July 28, 2007).

Pattee, Fred Lewis. "Fitz-Greene Halleck." *Century Readings for a Course in American Literature*. New York: The Century Co., 1919.

Taylor, Bayard and Marie Hansen Taylor. *Critical Essays and Literary Notes*. New York: G.P. Putnam's Sons, 1880.

Tierney, John. "An Ode to Fitz." *New York Times* (June 22, 1997).

Wilson, James Grant. *The Memorial History of the City of New York*. New York: New York History Company, 1893.

Wilson, James Grant and James Fiske. *Appleton's Cyclopaedia of American Biography*. New York: D. Appleton, 1888.

Wilson, James Grant. *The Life and Letters of Fitz-Greene Halleck.* New York: D. Appleton, 1869.

Wilson, James Grant. *Bryant and His Friends.* New York: Fords, Howard and Hulbert, 1886.

Rokeby

"La Bergerie/Rokeby." *Historic American Buildings Survey NY-5623.* Library of Congress and Oral History: J. Winthrop Aldrich, Rokeby.

Scott, Walter. *Rokeby.* Edinburgh: John Ballantyne and Co., 1813.

Springside

Lossing, Benson. *Vassar College and Its Founder.* New York: C.A. Alvord, 1867.

"Ode to Springside." *Poughkeepsie Eagle* (June 12, 1852).

Founder's Day

Lossing, Benson. *Vassar College and Its Founder.* New York: C.A. Alvord, 1867.

Haight, Elizabeth Hazelton. *The Autobiography and Letters of Matthew Vassar.* New York: Oxford University Press, 1916.

Myron Benton

Burroughs, John. "Myron B. Benton." *The Magazine of Poetry Volume II.* Buffalo: Charles Wells Moulton, 1890.

Benton, Myron. *Songs of the Webutuck.* Poughkeepsie: A.V. Haight Company, 1906.

Joel Benton

Benton, Joel. "The Winter Woods." *Poughkeepsie News-Telegraph* (February, 19, 1898).

Benton, Joel. "Grandmother's Garden." *St. Nicholas Magazine,* 1903.

Benton, Joel. *Persons and Places.* New York: Broadway Publishing Company, 1905.

Benton, Charle E. *Troutbeck: A Dutchess County Homestead.* Dutchess County Historical Society, 1916.

"The Civic Exercises." *Poughkeepsie Daily Eagle* (July 27, 1888).

Dyer, Edward Oscar. *Gnadersee, the Lake of Grace.* Boston: Pilgrim Press, 1903.

"Obituary - Joel Benton." *Poughkeepsie Daily Eagle* (September 16, 1911), *Poughkeepsie Sunday Courier* (September 17, 1911).

Rickert, Edith and Jessie Patton. *American Lyrics.* Garden City: Doubleday, 1912.

Stevenson, Elizabeth. *Days and Deeds.* Garden City: Doubleday, 1906.

Horatio Nelson Powers

Croaker, Samuel R. *The Literary World: A Monthly Review of Current Literature.* S.R. Croaker, 1887.

"Horatio Nelson Powers." *The Magazine of Poetry and Literary Review Volume I.* Buffalo: Charles Wells Moulton, 1889.

Orcutt, Samuel. *A History of Stratford and the City of Bridgport, CT.* New Haven: Tuttle, Morehouse and Taylor, 1886.

Powers, Horatio Nelson. *Poems, Early and Late.* Chicago: Jansen, McClurg and Company, 1876.

Powers, Horatio. Nelson. *Ten Years of Song: Poems.* Boston: D. Lothrop Company, 1887.

Edward Hazen Parker

Crosby, Howard. "Letter to the Editor." *New York Times* (January 13, 1898).

"Death of Dr. Parker." *Poughkeepsie News-Telegraph* (November 14, 1896), *Poughkeepsie Daily Eagle* (November 10, 1896).

Dr. Edward H. Parker is Dying." *New York Times* (November 8, 1896).

MacCracken, Henry. *Blithe Dutchess.* New York: Hastings House, 1958.

"Notes." *The Magazine of Poetry*, 1892.

Parker, Edward Hazen. *"Life's Race Well Run" With a Sketch of Its*

History. Poughkeepsie: Hiram S. Wiltsie, 1884.

Shrady, George F. "Obituary." *Medical Record* (July-December 1896) Volume 50.

"Tract." Western Reserve Historical Society, 1888.

Ward, David B. "Memorial of Dr. Edward H. Parker." Transactions of the Medical Society of the State of New York. 1897.

Wallace Bruce

Adams, Arthur G. *The Hudson River in Literature.* SUNY Albany, 1980.

Bruce, Wallace. *From the Hudson to the Yosemite.* New York: American News Company, 1884.

Bruce, Wallace. *Old Homestead Poems.* New York: Harper, 1888.

"Eastman College Anniversary." *Poughkeepsie Daily Eagle* (September 20, 1884).

Edwards, David Herschell. *One Hundred Modern Scottish Poets.* Self-published, 1883.

"Our Dead Heroes." *Poughkeepsie Daily Eagle* (June 1, 1880).

"Reception to Mr. Bruce." *Poughkeepsie Daily Eagle* (October 28, 1893).

"Wallace Bruce." *Poughkeepsie Sunday Courier* (June 11, 1893).

"Wallace Bruce on the Hudson." *Poughkeepsie Daily Eagle* (October 19, 1893).

Wallace, Alexander. *The Heather in Lore, Lyric and Lay.* New York: A. T. De La Mare, 1903.

William Harloe

"Failure of William Harloe." *New York Times* (August 28, 1879).

Harloe, Charles Bruce. *Harloe-Kelso Genealogy.* Winchester: Pifer Printing Co., 1943.

Harloe, William. "Letter to the Editor: The Future of Vassar College." *Poughkeepsie Daily Eagle* (June 24, 1880).

"Old Houses: 16 Davies Place." *Poughkeepsie Journal* (February 15, 1948).

"Obituary - Harloe." *Poughkeepsie Evening Enterprise* (Februrary 2, 1891), *Poughkeepsie News-Telegraph* (Februrary 7, 1891), *Poughkeepsie Daily Eagle* (February 2, 1891), *Courier* (February 1, 1891).

Josh Billings

Benton, Joel. "Reminiscences of Eminent Lecturers." *Harper's Magazine* (March 1898).

Benton, Joel. *Persons and Places.* New York: Broadway Publishing Company, 1905.

Billings, Josh and Thomas Nast. *The Complete Works of Josh Billings (pseud.).* New York: G.W. Dillingham, 1876.

"Henry W. Shaw." *The National Cyclopedia of American Biography.* 1896.

"Josh Billings." *Poughkeepsie News Press* (May 26, 1884; July 9, 1885; May 26, 1884; November 28, 1885) *Poughkeepsie News Telegraph* (November 14, 1885); *Poughkeepsie Daily Eagle* (December 11, 1884; October 15, 1885); *Poughkeepsie Courier* (November 5, 1899; January 6, 1895).

Myers, Helen. "Humorist Josh Billings." *Poughkeepsie Journal* (January 31, 1954).

Ridpath, John Clark. *The Ridpath Library of Universal Literature.* Philadelphia: Avil Printing Company, 1903.

Riley, James Whitcomb. *The Old Soldier's Story: Poems and Prose Sketches.* Bobbs-Merrill Company, 1915.

Smith, Francis Shubael. *Life and Adventures of Josh Billings.* New York: G. W. Carleton, 1883.

George W. Davids

"Obituary." *Poughkeepsie Daily Eagle* (February1 and February 5, 1894), *Pougheepsie News-Telegraph* (February 3, 1894).

"Sign of Spring." *Poughkeepsie Daily Eagle* (March 4, 1882).

Vassar College

Book of Vassar Verse: Reprints from Vassar Miscellany Monthly

(1894-1916) Vassar Miscellany Monthly, 1916.

Irwin, Wallace. *The Shame of Colleges*. (New York: Curtis Publishing Company, 1906).

Maar, Harry V. "Light After Darkness." *Poughkeepsie Daily Eagle* (October 2, 1896).

Vassar College 75th Anniversary Songbook. G. Shirmer, Inc., 1940.

Maria Mitchell

Babbitt, Mary King. *Maria Mitchell as Her Students Knew Her*. Poughkeepsie, 1919.

Bergland, Renee. *Maria Mitchell and the Sexing of Science*. Becon Press, 2008.

Kendall, Phebe Mitchell. *Maria Mitchell: Life, Letters and Journals*. Boston: Lee and Shephard, 1896.

Lankford, John and Ricky L. Slavings, *American Astronomy: Community, Careers, and Power 1859-1940*. University of Chicago Press, 1997.

"Maria Mitchell at Vassar" *Poughkeepsie Daily Eagle* (November 8, 1889).

"Obituary" *Poughkeepsie Daily Eagle* (June 29, 1889).

Taylor, James Monroe and Elizabeth Haight. *Vassar*. New York: Oxford University Press, 1915.

Vassar Miscellany, Volume 16. Vassar College, 1886.

Wright, Helen. *Sweeper in the Sky*. New York: MacMillan, 1949.

Wood, Frances Ann. *Earliest Years at Vassar: Personal Recollections*. Vassar College Press, 1909.

Edna St. Vincent Millay

Book of Vassar Verse: Reprints from Vassar Miscellany Monthly (1894-1916) Vassar Miscellany Monthly, 1916.

Daniels, Elizabeth. "Edna St. Vincent Millay." *Vassar College Encyclopedia,* February 2007.

Epstein, Daniel. *What My Lips Have Kissed: The Loves and Love*

Poems of Edna St. Vincent Millay. New York: MacMillan, 2002.

Milford, Nancy. *Savage Beauty: The Life of Edna St. Vincent Millay.* New York: Random House, 2001.

Millay, Edna St. Vincent and Holly Peppe (ed.) *Early Poems of Edna St. Vincent Millay.* New York: Penguin Group, 1998.

Riverview Academy

"Riverview Annual Hop." *Poughkeepsie Daily Eagle* (February 25, 1897).

"Riverview Hop." *Poughkeepsie Daily Eagle* (March 1, 1897).

Poughkeepsie Regatta

"Joyous Celebration." *Poughkeepsie Daily Eagle* (June 26, 1897).

Lyon, Henry Adelbert (ed.). *Cornell Verse.* Andrus and Church, 1901.

Lundin, John W. and Stephen J. "Cornell's Influence on Washington and West Coast Rowing." *www.rowinghistory.net.* Friends of Rowing History 2005.

Poole, Murray Edward. *A Short Historical of Cornell University.* Ithaca: Cornell University Press, 1916.

"Poughkeepsie Regatta." *Poughkeepsie Sunday Courier* (June 28, 1896) (June 16, 1940).

Rice, Wallace. *The Athlete's Garland: A Collection of Verse of Sport and Pastime.* Chicago: A.C. McClurg and Company, 1905.

Waterman, Thomas Hewitt et al. *Cornell University: A History.* New York: University Publishing Society, 1905.

Rhinebeck, the Beautiful

Hammick, J.T. *Rhinebeck, the Beautiful.* Rhinebeck: Rhinebeck Gazette Printing Office, 1899.

Dutchess County Courthouse

"The New Court House." *Poughkeepsie Daily Eagle* (November 22, 1901).

"The Old Court House."*Poughkeepsie Daily Eagle* (January 28, 1902).

"Old Memories How They Cling." *Poughkeepsie News-Telegraph* (February 1, 1902).

"Some Short Notes." *Poughkeepsie Daily Eagle* (January 31, 1902).

"The Vandal." *Poughkeepsie News-Telegraph* (February 8, 1902), (July 20, 1889).

John Jay Chapman

Chapman, John Jay. *Songs and Poems*. New York: Charles Scribner's Sons, 1919.

Chapman, John Jay. *Unbought Spirit: A John Jay Chapman Reader.* Champaign: University of Illinois Press, 1998.

"Chapman Is Killed in Aeroplane Fight." *New York Times* (June 25, 1916).

Howe, M.A. DeWolfe (ed.). "Letters from John Jay Chapman." *Harper's Magazine* (September 1937 and October 1937).

Thomas, Lately. *The Astor Orphans: A Pride of Lions*. New York: W. Morrow, 1971.

Wilson, Edmund. *The Triple Thinkers*. New York: Harcourt, Brace and Company, 1938.

Margaret Chanler Aldrich

Aldrich, Margaret Chanler. *The Horns of Chance*. London: Elkin Matthews, 1914.

Aldrich, Margaret Chanler. "The Soldier to His Mother" *New York Times* (March 24, 1918).

Aldrich, Margaret Chanler. "Victor Emmanuel Chapman" *Harvard Alumni Bulletin* Volume 19 (1916).

Aldrich, Margaret Chanler. Unpublished poems. Rokeby Collection.

Thomas, Lately. *The Astor Orphans: A Pride of Lions*. New York: W. Morrow, 1971.

Joel E. Spingarn

Maloney, Russell. "Accent on Clem." *The New Yorker* (March 21, 1936).

Smith, Gene. "Tales from Troutbeck." *Hudson Valley Magazine* (August 2004).

Spingarn, Joel Elias. *The New Hesperides and Other Poems.* Sturgis and Walton Company, 1911.

Spingarn, Joel Elias. "The New Criticism." *The New Criticism: An Anthology of Modern Aesthetics and Literary Criticism.* New York: Prentice-Hall, 1930.

Stevenson, Benton Egbert. *Book of Home Verse American and English 1580-1918.* New York: Henry Holt, 1918.

College Hill

"To a Hill." *Poughkeepsie Sunday Courier* (December 19, 1920).

Kimlin Cider Mill

Fisher, Katherine. "Owner Explains Process of Making Sweet Cider." *Poughkeepsie Courier* (October 1, 1939).

"Golden Nectar Made from Fruit of Famous Orchards." *Poughkeepsie Courier* (December 1, 1935).

MacCracken, Henry Noble. *The Hickory Limb.* New York: Charles Scribner's Sons, 1950.

Marshall, Joseph R. "Kimlins Are Among Last Sheep Herdsmen in Dutchess." *Poughkeepsie New Yorker* (July 8, 1951).

Myers, Helen. "Cider Mill Owner Shares Stories." *Poughkeepsie New Yorker* (February 12, 1956).

Myers, Helen. "Volens et Valens." *Poughkeepsie New Yorker* (February 8, 1948).

"Ralph Kimlin Dies at 82" *Poughkeepsie Journal* (May 4, 1969).

Innisfree

Collins, Lester. *Innisfree: An American Garden.* New York: Saga Press, Inc., 1994.

"Garden Notebook; In Mystical Innisfree." *NY Times* (July 1, 1994).

Locust Grove

Poughkeepsie Journal Jan. 31, 1965; Aug. 20, 1967; Dec. 23, 1975.

Frank S. Dickerson

Dickerson, Frank S. *Consider the Angels: Collected Poetry.* Truro, MA: Pamet River Press, 1996.

Fala

Ward, Geoffrey C. *Closest Companion: The Unknown Story of the Intimate Friendship Between Franklin Roosevelt and Margaret Suckley.* Boston: Houghton Mifflin, 1995.

Franklin Delano Roosevelt

Noonan, Peggy. "Confessions of a White House Speechwriter." *New York Times Magazine* (October 15, 1989).

Eleanor Roosevelt

Jenkins, Roy and Richard E. Neustadt. *Franklin Delano Roosevelt.* New York: Macmillan, 2003.

Pottker, Janice. *Sara and Eleanor.* New York: Macmillan, 2004.

Roosevelt, Eleanor. *Autobiography of Eleanor Roosevelt.* DaCapo Press, 1992.

Chanler Chapman

Boyle, Robert H. "Step In and Enjoy the Turmoil." *Sports Illustrated* (June 13, 1977).

Chapman, Chanler. "Memoirs, July 1970." *The Barrytown Explorer* (January-March 1982).

Middleton, Daniel. "The Chanler Chapman Show." *About Town* (Winter 2005).

Philip, Cynthia Owen. "The Lives of Barrytown - Parts 1-4" *About Town* (Summer 2006; Fall 2006; Winter 2006; Spring 2007).

Smith, George A. "His Irrespressible Spirit, His Vital Enthusiasm." *The Barrytown Explorer* (April 1982).

Correction to 2007 Year Book (Volume 86) *Dutchess Community College: The 50th Anniversary - A Special Issue*: C.B. Schmidt was the first Chairman of the Board of Trustees for Dutchess Community College, not Joseph Jiudice as was incorrectly stated on page 41.

Illustrations

(page 1) **Henry Livingston:** *A Mouse in Henry Livingston's House*: a website by Mary Van Deusen; www.iment.com.

(page 9) **William Wilson:** *Poems* by William Wilson (Benson Lossing, Editor) 1881.

(page 16) **Wildercliff:** HABS-NY, 14 Rhineb. v. 3 (taken after 1933).

(page 22) **Fitz-Greene Halleck:** *A Memorial* by Frederick S. Cozzens, 1868.

(page 31) **Rokeby:** *The Hudson from the Wilderness to the Sea* by Benson Lossing, 1866.

(page 33) **Springside:** Painting by Henry Gritten (1867).

(pages 36 and 39) **Bust of Matthew Vassar, Vassar Main Building:** "What are They Doing at Vassar?" by H.H. McFarland, *Scribner's Magazine*, August 1871.

(page 40) **Myron Benton:** *Songs of the Webutuck* by Myron Benton, 1906.

(page 48) **Joel Benton:** *Memories of the Twilight Club* by Joel Benton and Charles F. Wingate, 1910.

(page 57) **Horatio Nelson Powers:** "Literary Chicago" by William M. Payne, *The New England Magazine*: Volume 13, Issue 6.

(page 62) **Dover Stone Church:** *General History of Dutchess County from 1609 to 1876* by Philip Henry Smith, 1877.

(page 63) **Dr. Edward Hazen Parker:** *Commemorative Biographical Record of Dutchess County*, 1897.

(page 67-68) **Ice Yachting:** "Ice Yachting on the Hudson" by Charles H. Farnham, *Scribner's Magazine*, August 1881.

(page 70) **Wallace Bruce:** Collection of Adriance Memorial Library.

(page 80) **Eastman Business College Exterior:** Robert N. Dennis Collection, New York Public Library.

(page 84) **William Harloe:** Mayoral Portrait, 1879, Poughkeepsie City Hall.

(page 85-86) **Churches built by Harloe:** *Pougheepsie Daily Eagle*: June 29, 1895; September 14, 1895; September 28, 1895; October 26, 1895.

(page 87 and 89) **Josh Billings:** "Reminiscences of Eminent Lecturers" by Joel Benton; *Harper's Magazine*, March 1898; Josh Billing's *Allminax* 1871.

(page 91) **George Davids:** *Poughkeepsie Daily Eagle*: 2/1/1894.

(page 95) **Vassar College:** *50th Anniversary of the Opening of Vassar College*: A Record (October 10-13, 1915).

(page 103) **Vassar Girls:** University of Iowa Special Collections; Repath Chautauqua Collection; date unknown.

(page 105) **Maria Mitchell** (1872): courtesy of Special Collections, Vassar College Libraries.

(page 108) **Vassar College Observatory 1879**: courtesy of Special Collections, Vassar College Libraries.

(page 111) **Edna St. Vincent Millay:** Library of Congress Portrait Photograph.

(page 115) **Riverview Academy:** Postcard, 1911. Private Collection.

(page 118) **Stanford Crew between 1910 and 1915:** Library of Congress Prints and Photographs Division.

(page 120) **Intercollegiate Race 1914:** Library of Congess Prints and Photographs Division.

(page 122) **Cornell Crew 1897:** New York Public Library: The Pagaent of America Collection.

(page 126) **Map of Rhinebeck 1890:** L.R. Burleigh, Troy, New York: Library of Congress Geography and Maps Division.

(page 130) **Dutchess County Courthouse:** Dutchess County Historical Society Collection.

(page 133) **John Jay Chapman:** Rokeby Collection (courtesy of J. Winthrop Aldrich).

(pages 143, 146, 149) **Margaret Chanler Aldrich:** photo from Rokeby Collection (courtesy of J. Winthrop Aldrich); photo of Victor Chapman from *Letters from France by Victor Chapman 1917*; portrait of Margaret Livingston Chanler from *Town and Country* Magazine 1903.

(page 151) **Joel Spingarn:** circa 192_, Library of Congress.

(page 156) **College Hill Conservatory:** *Poughkeepsie: Queen City of the Hudson River*, L.M. Hermance, 1909.

(page 158) **Kimlin Cider Mill:** courtesy of Cider Mill Friends of Open Space and Historic Preservation, Inc.

(page 162) **Annette Young:** courtesy of Locust Grove Historic Site.

(page 165) **Frank Dickerson:** courtesy of Fort Homestead Association.

(pages 171, 173) **FDR, Eleanor Roosevelt:** FDR Presidential Library and Museum.

(page 176) **Chanler Chapman:** Rokeby Collection (courtesy of J. Winthrop Aldrich).

Historical Societies of Dutchess County

Amenia Historical Society
P.O. Box 22
Amenia, NY 12501

Beacon Historical Society
P.O. Box 89
Beacon, NY 12508

Clinton Historical Society
P.O. Box 122
Clinton Corners, NY 12514

Dover Historical Society
N. Nellie Hill Road
Dover Plains, NY 12522

East Fishkill Historical
Society
P.O. Box 245
Hopewell Junction, NY 12533

Fishkill Historical Society
P.O. Box 133
Fishkill, NY 12524

Hyde Park Historical Society
P.O. Box 182
Hyde Park, NY 12538

LaGrange Historical Society
P.O. Box 112
LaGrangeville, NY 12540

Little Nine Partners
Historical Society
P.O. Box 243
Pine Plains, NY 12567

North East Historical Society
P.O. Box 727
Millerton, NY 12546

Historical Society of Quaker
Hill and Pawling, Inc.
P.O. Box 99
Pawling, NY 12546

Pleasant Valley Historical
Society
P.O. Box 309
Pleasant Valley, NY 12569

Egbert Benson Historical
Society of Red Hook
P.O. Box 1813
Red Hook, NY 12571

Rhinebeck Historical Society
P.O. Box 291
Red Hook, NY 12572

Museum of Rhinebeck
History
P.O. Box 816
Rhinebeck, NY 12572

Roosevelt/Vanderbilt
Historical Association
P.O. Box 235
Hyde Park, NY 12538

Stanford Historical Society
P.O. Box 552
Bangall, NY 12506

Union Vale Historical Society
P.O. Box 100
Verbank, NY 12585

Wappingers Historical
Society
P.O. Box 974
Wappingers Falls, NY 1259

Town of Washington
Historical Society
551 Route 343
Millbrook, NY 12545

Municipal Historians of Dutchess County

County Historian:

Stanley Mersand, 170 Washingston Street, Poughkeepsie 12601

City Historians:

Beacon: Robert Murphy,1 Municipal Plaza, Beacon 12508
Poughkeepsie: George Lukacs, PO Box 300, Poughkeepsie 12602

Village and Town Historians:

Amenia: Arlene Pettersen, 82 Separate Rd., Amenia 12501 • **Beekman**: Thom Usher, 96 Hillside Road, Poughquag 12570 • **Clinton:** Craig Marshall, 1375 Centre Road, Rhinebeck 12572 • **Dover:** Donna Hearn, 126 E. Duncan Hill Rd., Dover Plains 12522 • **East Fishkill**: Caroline Plage, 330 Rte.376, Hopewell Jct. 12533 • **Fishkill (Town)**: Willa Skinner, 807 Rte. 52, Fishkill 12524 • **Fishkill (Village**): Karen Hitt, 91 Main Street, Fishkill 12524 • **Hyde Park**: Ave Clark, 64 Mill Road, Hyde Park 12538 • **LaGrange:** Georgia Herring-Trott, 120 Stringham Rd., Lagrangeville 12540 • **Milan**: Patrick Higgins, Milan Town Hall, 20 Wilcox Circle, Milan 12571 • **Millbrook:** David Greenwood, 510 Sharon Turnpike, Millbrook, 12545 • **Millerton:** Diane Thompson, PO Box 528, Millerton 12546 • **North East:** Diane Thompson, 516 Maple Ave., Millerton 12546 • **Pawling (Town)**: Robert Reilly, 160 Charles Colman Blvd., Pawling 12564 • **Pawling (Village):** Drew Nicholson, 18 Valley Drive, Pawling 12564 • **Pine Plains**: Little Nine Partners Historical Society, PO Box 243 Pine Plains 12567 • **Pleasant Valley:** Fred Schaeffer, Town Hall, Route 44, Pleasant Valley 12569 • **Poughkeepsie (Town)**: Jean Murphy, 1 Overocker Rd., Poughkeepsie 12603 • **Red Hook**: J. Winthrop Aldrich, 109 S. Broadway, Red Hook 12571 • **Rhinebeck (Town and Village):** Nancy Kelly, 80 E. Market St., Rhinebeck 12572 • **Stanford:** Dorothy Burdick, 26 Town Hall Road, Stanfordville 12581 • **Tivoli:** Bernie Tieger, 96 Broadway, Tivoli 12583 • **Unionvale**: Fran Wallin, 249 Duncan Rd., LaGrangeville 12540 • **Wappingers Falls (Town):** Janice Hilderbrand, 20 Middlebush Rd., Wappingers Falls 12590 • **Wappingers Falls (Village):** Brenda Von Berg, Town Hall, 2 South Avenue, Wappingers Falls, 12590 • **Washington**: David Greenwood, 10 Reservoir Drive, Millbrook 12545

Dutchess County Historical Society

Founded in 1914, Dutchess County Historical Society is a research, archival and educational organization dedicated to the discovery, preservation and dissemination of the history of Dutchess County. As the only county-wide agency of its kind, the Historical Society is an active leader in the collection and safe-keeping of artifacts, manuscripts and other priceless treasures of the past.

The Historical Society has been instrumental in the preservation and continuing management of two Revolutionary era landmarks, the Clinton House and Glebe House in the City of Poughkeepsie. In addition, it operates the Franklin A. Butts Research Library as well as publishing a newsletter, annual Year Book and special journals.

The Historical Society also maintains photograph and object collections, mounts changing exhibits and sponsors historical trips, lectures, seminars, house tours, history awards, and books sales as well as providing leadership and support for many other collaborative heritage and history education projects.

Historian and writer **HOLLY WAHLBERG** is a graduate of Boston University, Columbia University and the Sotheby's of London Design Education Program. Currently, she lives in the City of Poughkeepsie where she has been active in a number of preservation and history awareness projects.